SURVIVING THE STORM

(How to Embrace Your Pain & Grow Through Adversity)

Jennie Matthias

Author: Jennie Matthias Title: Surviving The Storm

ISBN: 978-1916030121 Category: Mental-Health/Self-Help/Addiction Publisher: Breakfree Forever Publishing

CONTENTS

INTRODUCTION

All the things that I have experienced throughout this lifetime have led me to where I am at this moment, and I would not be the person I am today without the experiences that I had. I now see those moments as priceless gifts that were passed my way to help strengthen me. There are probably millions of ways in which a person can change their circumstances with the view of creating a better life for themselves and then others. What I share with you are just a few that have helped me on my journey; each of them 100% positive that have also given me great results. Today, my mind focuses only on the positive, which is a huge step from how I used to be. For me to be able to survive the life I had been through, I slowly took notes and created a SURVIVAL mechanism that still works for me to this day. I share those notes with you now in the hope that it will also do the same for you.

My greatest wish is that this book inspires a person into positive action, where their vision of themselves can be viewed in a positive manner. This book is all about SURVIVAL and offers several options of how to overcome certain situations by just doing and viewing things differently, getting involved and stepping out of your comfort zone once and a while. It is a series of stories and information from those in the know that have grown through the darkest parts of their life to go on to inspire others to do the same.

This book is for those that have survived parental rejection, violent upbringings, overcome drug and alcohol abuse, anyone with low self-esteem, stuck at a crossroads in life or just simply looking to be inspired. This book is about self-discovery and positive outcomes. It's about offering a glimpse into how an optimistic mindset can enable you to have a more meaningful, rewarding, and more fulfilling life.

FOREWORD

My beautiful friend Jenny is like the warmest, most positively loving hurricane to blow through your life. From a background of adversity and pain to excess and fame, this woman has weathered it all. Today. She uses this lifetime experience to champion Love in all it's forms. A man told me one time that humans are motivated by two things- Love & Fear, when you practice one, the other disappears. This woman practices Love, BELIEVE! [Actor Michael Smiley]

ABOUT THE AUTHOR

Born out of wedlock in the late 1950s to an uneducated Jamaican immigrant father and violent Irish mother, the eldest of six siblings from mixed parentage, life was always going to be "interesting." Growing up with dysfunction as the norm, of course, had added trauma. When money was dry, moods ran high, and as the oldest, I would be the sounding board and punching bag for my mother's aggression. Respite came by way of children's homes, where years were spent learning new rules and acquiring a better education, life skills, and outlook. When forced to go back to the parental home at the age of 9, the reign of terror started where it left off. It was visible for all to see that I was a troubled child, unsurprisingly expulsion from schools followed. My teenage years were fraught with fear at home and a fragmented education due to the various schools I was placed in left me confused and despondent. At 15, I left home and went my own way. At 22, an unexpected audition saw me shoot to fame in the '80s where I was courted by all forms of media, especially TV and Radio. This newfound fame also opened the doors to free drugs, drink and partying, and what was once recreational soon became habitual. After the band eventually split, I unwittingly pursued the life of an addict, ditching everyone I knew, replacing old friends with those that could supply my habit. After years of self-abuse, I finally cleaned my act up. Since then, I have taught drug awareness in schools, created shows encompassing creative sketches about those experiences, founded a drug awareness charity for which I was honoured as a community champion, have mentored young people sharing contacts and knowledge to enhance their growth and have come back full circle to live performance, writing, singing, and touring. My life experience has enabled me to become an authority on surviving various forms of trauma, and I now feel that the remaining stages of my life will be about assisting those that are hesitant and lacking the confidence they need when stuck at the crossroads trying to cope with their pain. Having learnt to embrace the pain of the past, I feel confident that the tools I have acquired are beneficial to all who are seeking positive change within their lives. Those experiences have enabled me to find my life's purpose, which is aimed at educating, empowering, and strengthening the minds of those who have gone through similar hardships.

I am a survivor of numerous traumas that life has either thrown my way or that have been self-afflicted. Since I have gone through these and have managed to come out the other side virtually unscathed, I feel confident enough to share the survival techniques that have kept me moving onwards and upwards, leading me to pursue my life's purpose, which is teaching survivors how to embrace their pain so as they can then go on to use it as a tool for Self-Development, not only for themselves, but others also. I believe that the cure for coping with pain and sorrow is to embrace it by looking deeper into why it exists in your life at all. Only when I started to look deeper into why certain things in my life were not moving at the speed in which I would have liked did I realise that I was allowing my negative past to affect what I did as a grown up. My response to how I had been treated as a child was bitterness, anger, and hatred, which all carry low vibration feelings. My childhood was filled with terror and fear and, of course, this would have an effect on me mentally, causing all sorts of painful situations to branch out from those uncomfortable experiences of the past.

I choose to teach experientially rather than academically what it takes to survive in a world like ours. Teaching from an experiential standpoint usually offers comfort for those looking to heal themselves from certain traumatic experiences, addictions, and struggles. People going through all types of adversity usually find themselves drawn to those that have gone through similar hardships and often use their knowledge as a way to inspire themselves into positive mental and physical action. I have recently created a project called 'SHOW & GROW' aimed at those who are struggling to cope with their pain and anyone seeking positive change within their life. My aim is to make one million people realise their worth by 2020. I aim to change lives for the better.

"Extraordinary people survive under the most terrible circumstances, and they become more extraordinary because of it"

[Robertson Davies]

SURVIVE

My mother used to say to me
'I hate you; you are ugly'
and for years amidst the tears
I'd let those words she said define me
coupled with the violence
there was not a single way
a girl like me would ever get the chance
to grow up normally.
For years, I took to heart
those words of negativity
but thankfully today
I look at life - more philosophically
and as I share my story with you all
I've come to realise
it's got to be a miracle
how I've managed to survive
physically and mentally
my mind and body still intact.
The fact that I'm still here to tell the tale
means something out there's got my back
and I'm amazed at how I got through
every grim ordeal.
I sometimes have to pinch myself

to see if it's all real
and when I look back on those years
when hard knocks ran rivers of tears
the image of those days is sad
but time has healed the pain
and I'm so glad.
I went through
all the beatings and abuse
for if I had not done it
I could not share this with you.
Without all that experience
how could I ever show
people who had been through similar hardship
how they too can grow.
I honestly believe
it was all meant to be
to turn me into the person
that you can now see.
It made me a master
in my chosen field
the school of hard-knocks-isn't-fiction
is real.
And as you endure
every pain, every hurt
you grow up thinking
that you have no worth.
Your pain turns to sorrow
a burden like a curse
until one-day your bubble
changes and bursts.

Then all of a sudden
the scales from your eyes
are lifted and then
you soon realise
that you are much more
than what one person thinks of you
and there starts your journey
towards a new avenue.
And each step you tread
along the new road
brings clarity of mind
as you shed every load
and the people you meet
are different from those
in the past who would seek
to stunt you in growth.
But as you can see
I'm still alive
I've got a master's degree
on how to survive.
My journey has brought me
to a single conclusion
'where there's a problem
there's also a solution.'
So I've set up a programme
it's called SHOW & GROW
to help raise the vibration
to those who don't know
that they have a greatness
inside them of worth

and it's my job to show them
survival on earth.
I didn't go through that life
with the pains I endured
just to cower in corners
afraid to be heard.
NO, I used to do that
but not any more
coz my life now has a purpose
and I'm ready for war
and all who I help
with what I now know
will benefit greatly
from this SHOW & GROW.
It's a programme for those
seeking positive change
who are stuck at a crossroads
trying to cope with their pain.
Well, I am a master at showing them how
to grow through adversity
coz I can now
honestly say, I am grateful today
for the life that I had
and would not ever change.
Our world needs some leaders
to show them the light
and I am just one
that can help with that plight.
I now have the tools
to assist each survivor

with the aim of creating
a new breed of warrior.
My programme provides
the tools to keep going
created by those in the know
who are showing
how they have managed to cope with their pain
embrace every moment and live life again.
SHOW & GROW
is now my life's purpose
and all that I went through
was finally worth it.
It's all my life's work
and all that I think of.
SHOW & GROW will be
my Legacy of **LOVE.**

PREFACE

Before I start, I would like to introduce myself. My name is Jennie, and I am a Motivational Speaker, Self-Development Teacher, Professional Singer, and Founder of Show and Grow, which is something that I created to help educate, inspire, empower, and strengthen the minds of those who are struggling to cope through adversity. Show and Grow is about encouraging survivors to embrace their pain so as they can then go on to use it as a tool for self-development. Unlike many in my field, not only have I survived numerous traumas, but I have also managed to master the art of Live Performance on a global scale, both of which I have applied to Show & Grow, enabling me to offer a truly distinctive programme for anyone seeking positive change within their life. But do you know something? I honestly believe that traumatic experiences are gifts, passed our way to help strengthen us, so that we can then go on to become our greater selves. I also believe that if you are a person that has experienced any form of trauma within your lifetime, then you are in the know, and those who know teach, and those who teach experientially are best placed to help the human race evolve. Show & Grow is about evolution; it's about creating the new breed of warrior, and it's about raising the vibration of every single being on this planet. Show & Grow is simply about one thing... LOVE.

CHAPTER 1

MY STORY

In 1957, I was born out of wedlock to an Irish/English Mother and Jamaican father, both of which were poorly educated. My early years were spent in poverty, and by the time I was three, my Mother bore 3 children. Bernadette, who was originally the eldest, died before I was born, then came me, and a year later my little sister Elaine. When money was tight, moods ran high, and tolerance of anything slightly annoying to my Mother became very low. It was on one of these low days that Elaine had been crying incessantly, and her high-pitched tones were too much for my Mother's short temper. She just snapped, grabbed a pillow, put it over her face while I looked on in helpless horror, terror, fear, anger, and sadness. After a short while, Elaine cried no more, nor would I ever see or play with her ever again in this lifetime. I was left alone with a Mother aware that I had witnessed her actions and, boy, I was going to pay in later years for that involuntary intrusion.

My mother (Margaret McKeown), fell pregnant again and had two more children with my father Bill Matthias, Paul and Dorothy. It became apparent to Social Services that this was not an ideal setting for children to grow up in, so we were taken away and temporarily put into a convent in Mill Hill. The convent was cold and uncaring, and the majority of Nuns lacked compassion. They wore huge white hats and were scary and some of them too strict. Apart from Nurse Bruton, Sister Mary Theresa, and the animals, there was not much else I cared to remember about that place.

Eventually, we were moved to a children's home in Slough, where we met other boys and girls in a similar position to us. I remember being so happy there, and going to school was a joy. I loved reading and writing, and Auntie Alice who ran the home knew this and ordered my favourite comics once a week. When they arrived, I would lose myself in the storylines. Auntie Alice was a kind, gentle, compassionate woman, who made sure we went on holiday every year, indulge in Easter eggs at Easter and have a sack full of toys given to orphanage children by well-wishers, which really made our Xmas. It was a joyous household, and I learnt much about the positive side of life from being there. Our daily routines gave us stability; we were also taught to have good manners in a strict but loving way. We were free to be happy children. On reflection, I would say this place was our saving grace.

I was approximately 8 when the Social Services in their ignorance decided that we might benefit from going back to my mother's house, so we were given a trial weekend to see if it would work. Compared to the home, the place was dirty, and also there were more brothers and sisters from different fathers who were complete strangers to us. We moved in two weeks later, and from there on, my life turned to darkness. I would never see my beautiful Auntie Alice ever again.

The very large apartment was in Russell Square, on the top floor of an Edwardian or Georgian building. It was a scary place for me and nothing like the loving children's home I was forced to leave. I spent the following years there as a slave and a punch bag for my Mother's moods. I shopped and cooked, feeding six brothers and sisters, I washed their clothes and helped get them ready for school. Xmas was a sad, lonely time for me, and I lived in fear every day of having done something that might upset my mother. Primary school wasn't much better as I was constantly being mocked about the colour of my skin until, of course, one day I snapped, broke a girl's nose and was suspended… I never got mocked again after that.

Four years on and another change of scenery came when we moved to Camden Town. By now, I'm 12 years old, secondary school age and very much a wayward child. Being bullied at home by my mother and her new boyfriend drained me. I did, however, have a lot of friends in school. It was there I met a teacher who became a role model for me, and on one summer holiday, she asked to take me away to Norfolk to a cottage where I hung out and got to see different things. It was a respite from the house of horrors.

My mother was unable to keep a man, which was hardly surprising as her moods were very scary, and after a few more broken relationships, she finally had a nervous breakdown, which meant that my brothers and sisters from other fathers were put into children's homes. My sister Dorothy and brother Paul from my Father were offered the chance to go to Boarding Schools. My sister and I went to the one in Birmingham and, of course, we jumped at the opportunity to get away. It was there that I met the fabulous Polly Perkins, a gym instructor, another person who was to change my life positively. I finally felt free to be me, although I eventually blew it and got expelled, bringing me back to my mother's care, which was short-lived after she tried to raise her hands on me. For once in my life, I retaliated; she couldn't cope with that and put me back in a children's home in Borehamwood. I was just 15 then.

Once in Borehamwood, I found a job and went to work in a factory laboratory, which I liked. There, I fell in love with Billy, my first proper boyfriend. And by the age of 16, I moved in with him, we lived in Hendon, the relationship lasted 5 years, and the experiences with this man were lovely, but unfortunately, I was too young to commit and wanted to spread my wings. So sadly, I left him. I am happy to say that Billy is still in my life and one of my closest, dearest friends for which I am so very grateful for.

I then met Steve, became attached to him and hung with his friends who introduced me to recreational drugs, which went with being young, free, and punk. I lived a freedom I had never known before, and as this was during the punk era, anything went. Music, gigs, and fun were my pastime.

By the age of 21, I was given the opportunity to sing for someone who liked my speaking voice. They asked me to record a track, then word got out that I could sing, and within a year, I was on Top Of The Pops, plus other TV and radio shows globally. I toured nationally and abroad, where the following few years saw me living the pop star dream, simply enjoying life and the experiences that came with that. The music business, however, is rife with hangers-on and people that are all too ready to offer you some drug or another, and if you are the sort of person that is up for it [which I was], then you get suckered onto a dark path. Before long, I found myself hooked on heroin; what was once recreational turned habitual. Finally, the band ended and the following years saw my rapid demise.

As I got deeper into using, I could see and feel my self-respect and the respect that others once had for me going. Chris, my boyfriend at that time, suggested I go to Miami, the USA to try and clean up my act; which I did. I also had family there and used their place to clean up. While I was there, I had an unexpected hit that put me back in the charts and limelight; needless to say, I remained there for 2 years as that's where the work was for me.

I am now age 33 back in London and a few years down the line. Having managed to free myself from the clutches of Heroin, I started making music again with other people, and I fell hopelessly in love with Andrew, the bass player of a band I was in. Things looked like they were on the up as we were being pursued by a famous manager ready to sign us to a huge record label. I was living in Maida Vale, Andrew and I spent most of our time there, and we were really happy, writing songs and just being in love, until one day Andrew's clinical depression kicked in and, at the time, I knew nothing about depression or its effects on a person. Andrew was almost non-responsive, and after going back to his own flat to sort out his depression for a week, there was a knock on my door; it was the police who informed me that Andrew had taken his own life. He left a suicide note for whoever found him to contact me. I was devastated by this, and it's a strange thing that when you are in your moments of despair, the people you meet at that time are all too ready to feed you with uppers, downers, and such like. Soon after, I went back on heroin.

An old friend who was actually from the children's home in Slough heard what had happened to me and invited me to stay at the Buddhist Centre in Scotland to heal myself. She herself had taken up robes, and it was such an eye-opener for me. It was also the best thing that had happened to me in a long while. The experience took me on a spiritual quest, which turned my life around. I hung out with the Monks and Nuns and became very interested in spiritual philosophy, and although I was still in great pain due to the loss of Andrew, I also had a feeling that one day I would not feel that pain anymore and so engrossed myself in self-help books and things that would uplift the spirit. I was drawn to anything that calmed down my very being; I became thirsty for knowledge.

In 1999, I set up my own Drug Awareness charity called 'S-Teem,' using the arts as a tool to educate young people with the aim of preventing them going down a similar route to the one that I had once travelled. Much of my work and poetry was about those times on drugs, and I would go out and perform these sketches. On the strength of this, a teacher that happened to be in the audience invited us to come into her local school and teach drug awareness projects. It escalated from there and also paid us very well; it was the first insight I had into me being able to see my true worth due to my life's experience. I was putting my experiences to good use, and as I am also a creative person, I wrote a two-hour project for secondary and primary school children.

Current Date / Life's Purpose

After 60 years on this planet, I finally get why I went through all I did. I truly believe that my life was tailor-made for me to arrive at this point, so as I can play my part in helping the human race evolve. I feel blessed to have walked down, and through many dark paths, come out the other side and still be able to tell the tale. With all the experience I have acquired over my lifetime, I feel that I now have something so powerful to help humanity that it has become my greatest reason for getting out of bed each morning. It is now my 'Life's Purpose' to help as many people as I can to realise their full potential using the gifts of their own experiences.

Recently, I decided to create a project called 'SHOW & GROW,' which I believe is my life's purpose as everything that I have experienced thus far has led me to this point. As a survivor of physical, mental, and sexual abuse, I feel that I am in the perfect position to assist others who have gone through a similar situation. 'SHOW & GROW' is the tool that will make that happen. 'Show & Grow' was created by one who understands from the first-hand experience, how to rise from the ashes of darkness to then become a beacon of light for others.

The following categories within each chapter are just a few things that I applied on my journey to assist me in my survival here on earth. There were many more, but I have chosen to share the ones that helped me the most, and because my mission is to help raise the vibration of all beings on this planet, I felt it was important to share the most powerful lessons I took on board to heal myself and move on to become truly successful in my field.

CHAPTER 2

SOLUTION

"Leaders think and talk about the solutions, followers think and talk about the problems."

[Brian Tracy]

What follows in this chapter are various solutions that have helped me on my journey of recovery and survival. If you take in their meaning, then I believe that you too will be inspired to change whatever you wish for the better. I feel blessed and extremely grateful to be able to share them with you, and I hope that the contents within may inspire you to become the person you would most like to become. If you are reading this, then chances are that you want to either change something in your life or something about yourself. If this is so, then you have come to the right place, as the following chapters are all about finding solutions to life's varying problems and changing old habits, replacing them with new ones. Finding solutions to anything in life has long been my goal as I believe there are solutions to everything. Over the years, I have found myself in many predicaments, but guess what, I am still here to tell the tale and so I'm highly knowledgeable on the subject of survival; *KNOWLEDGE IS POWER*.

SACRIFICE

"If you don't sacrifice for what you want, what you want will be the sacrifice."

[Anonymous]

Sacrifice old habits to make room for ones more conducive to your wellbeing. The dictionary's definition of Sacrifice reads *'To sacrifice is to give up something valued for the sake of other considerations.'* If you truly mean business, then there are some things you are going to have to sacrifice for you to truly make that business work for you. Over a period of a few years, I chose to look at the things I was doing to myself with a view to replacing them with something better. I did this gradually and then stuck to it until I managed to master it and have since experienced positive results for doing so. I am not in any way suggesting that what I did is good for everyone, and even when I look at the list, I am astounded at how far I have come, but I can honestly say from personal experience that those things I did sacrifice gave me the space to replace those areas of my life with better choices. If someone had said to me 30 years ago that the following list is what you're going to stick to, I would never have believed them, but here I am, 30 years down the line and so much happier for making the following sacrifices.

WHAT I SACRIFICED TO REACH MY GOAL

SACRIFICED MEAT - *Replaced it with a plant-based diet.*

What this did to my health was incredible, not only did my weight drop without me even trying, but my skin looked a million times better. It knocked years off me; I felt lighter, healthier, and happier that I decided to stop being part of the problem that tortures and kills animals for their pallet. As I said, this change might not be for everyone, but for me, it had one of the most positive effects on my wellbeing. I am now my ideal weight with the most excellent skin along with incredible amounts of energy. One of the first things people notice about me is my energy and slender figure.

RESULTS: Fabulous skin: Clarity of mind: Healthy weight loss: Look and feel healthier: Have as much energy as I did when I was 21.

SACRIFICED TV - *Replaced it with reading books and writing*

To be honest, this act was not hard for me. Although my friends at that time could not get their heads around my decision, reading and writing were a refuge for me as a child in a children's home. I would sit for hours and read. I felt that TV was wasting my time and that I was being hypnotised by the content and particular shows that I simply loved to watch, but felt after doing so that I had wasted a good part of the day. I also used to get disturbed by some of the imagery on the screen and frustrated with the immaturity of the programmes. The TV I had was huge and just taking up too much space in my head and my apartment. It had to go, and since doing so, I cannot count the number of books I have read that have served me well and enabled me to understand life more and encourage a different way of thinking. I have never looked back, and even when I am at my friend's house on weekends, I go to my room, read, meditate, write, or do yoga. All of the above is far more beneficial to my wellbeing than just sitting on a sofa, wasting the hours away with things that have no substance; one of the best sacrifices I ever made.

RESULTS: Gained more knowledge due to reading: Written my first books: Written more in-depth poetry, which I perform live: Involved myself with the community a lot more; Visit friends; priceless.

SACRIFICED SMOKING - *Replaced it with taking care of my health*

As a person who has been smoking since the age of 10, I felt that I wouldn't have much time left on this planet if I were to keep this habit going, and so I made the decision to quit for good. I had tried in the past, but this time, I meant it from deep within, and I knew I would have to sacrifice all the things that came with letting go of that habit. I tried Vaping for a few weeks but didn't fancy becoming hooked on something I didn't understand. You will still need some willpower, but if your aim is true, then your will, will remain strong. And each day you refuse to subside is a day that you gain more personal strength and power until before you know it, you are no longer in the smokers' club. I was no longer prepared to sacrifice my life for a temporary hit of nicotine and all the nasty things that went with it like bad smells, messing with my taste buds, being anti-social, financial drainage, cravings and being a slave to something that is doing all it can to destroy my liver, lungs, and arteries. My health had become compromised, out of breath when running was the last straw as not being able to climb stairs and run was totally out of the question. I am happy to say that this is all behind me and I am able to run up and down the stairs as often as I care to.

RESULTS: More stamina, ability to run for miles, clothes and apartment smell sweeter, food tastes better, less haggard looking, fewer wrinkles, skin more plump and fresh knocking a good 7-8 years off my age, and I'm able to hit the high notes when singing.

SACRIFICED DRUGS - *Replaced it with a rigid gym routine*

When I decided to give up drugs, I did so with great gusto banning even aspirin. I noted that not only were the drugs taking their toll on my looks, but the company I chose to keep, that were associated with this behaviour had to go out of my life too. I finally realised that the drugs don't work anymore and that I would have to get myself off of them before they ravished me further. Whatever the reason I chose to take them, I realised that the reason would never go away until I found out what that was and addressed it soberly. I eventually stopped by weaning myself off for a very short period of a few weeks, then going cold turkey for the rest. I am not the type of person that would join such groups like NA or AA as I did not want to associate with other drug or ex-drug users. I had become a pitiful addict, and it was not a good look. Also, my respect for myself was non-existent, and my life was a sad mess, I wanted to get away from people like that. I decided to cut all ties and close the chapter on that part of my book, clean up my act and pursue the next chapter.

RESULT: Cleaner skin and clothing, better friends, less stress, fear or anxiety, regained my self-respect, became an authority on the subject of taking drugs and taught Drug Prevention in schools. Knocked years of my looks, joined the gym, inspired me to become an advocate for fitness and health, am also writing a book on the subject of *'coming off and staying clean'* the list of benefits due to that decision are simply endless.

SACRIFICED ALCOHOL - *Replaced it with water and fresh juices*

As you get older, you are unable to process alcohol like you once used to. I noticed that whenever I had gotten a little tipsy, I would feel it for so much longer than I did when I was younger. I also noticed its negative effects on my mood the morning after and how my thoughts would become quite dark and depressing. Another thing with alcohol is that it seems to be the favourite pastime for many, and as pubs are not quite my thing anymore, I figured that it was time to stop. I never ever had a problem with drink, but I did have a problem with the association of drink, and it has negative effects on my mind, body, health, and skin. I am happy to say that I now no longer drink, not even with dinner. Many of my friends still try and encourage me to have one, but saying no has since become a powerful game I play with myself. One that makes me feel very proud, and on top of that, most of my good friends respect my tenacity on this subject. Sacrificing alcohol and replacing it with water and fresh fruit juices has had a positive, visible effect on my skin and body.

RESULT: Softer healthier looking skin, NO hangovers, more money in my pocket, happier persona, positive mindset.

SACRIFICED LATE NIGHTS - *Replaced it with early nights*

Sacrificing late nights was easier said than done, but I managed to discipline myself to do it as I was on a mission to get my health and looks back. Also, I am a fan of daylight, and waking up late means that I miss the day and all the good properties that go with it like the Vitamin D and sense of wellbeing you get when you rise with the sun. When you get older, burning the candle at both ends takes its toll on your looks, health, finance, mood, and mental state. I found that it was taking me much longer to get my head around stuff the next day, having to go to work phase was uncomfortable and unproductive. There are still the odd times that I have late nights, but they only happen when I do performance poetry gigs and music shows, and even then I try to get an early slot so that I can do all I can to be in bed before midnight. I now have a routine of getting to bed by 9.00 pm the latest and up from 4.30 or 5.00 am to be in the gym for 6.00 am, which means making sure that I get every bit of sunlight throughout that day.

My life has changed dramatically since this sacrifice, and now it sees me getting up at least 4 - 6 hours earlier than I would have done before.

RESULT: Sacrificing late nights means that I am the first one in the gym, so I get the place almost to myself and better choice of the equipment. I have more hours to spare to write my books when I get back home, I have time to meditate and be more creative, and this is all before my friends rise in the morning. I am more prone to soak in nature, read books, and visit friends as there is much more time on my hands, but the vibe of being in the early bird club is just the most wonderful feeling, and I just will not look back on this. There is a whole new world with some seriously cool people up at that time in the day.

SACRIFICED SOCIALISING - *Replaced it with looking within*

When I made up my mind to stop socialising, it at first seemed like I was being a tad selfish, saying no all the time, but again socialising had long since felt like a chore, and often when I was asked out, I would think about what company would be there and was it worth me waking up late for or cutting myself off of a good night's sleep? Often socialising meant that I would have to leave my cosy apartment to make other people happy when, deep down, I would rather have been at home reading a book or writing. There was also drinking, partying, and smoking, etc. Then on top of that, it was virtually impossible to get home when it was truly late, and so I made the decision to sacrifice it all to remain indoors meditating and looking within. Staying in silence is the best medicine for those seeking peace for the soul, and I feel that is where I am at in my current years.

RESULTS: Sacrificing partying and socialising replacing it with searching for the meaning of life and looking within has resulted in me gaining more peace of mind, an eagerness to find a different social group that runs on a similar vibration to mine and turned me into an author and poet.

SOLITUDE

"Solitude is where one discovers one is not alone."

[Marty Rubin]

SOLITUDE is a must when you are at a crossroads in your life. It enables you to truly think about your situation. When you are alone with yourself, you only have yourself to deal with. You also have this mental chatter in your head [I call it analysing the situation], which may go on for days, weeks, months; see it as a clearing and a way of recognising some home truths. Get yourself a journal book to write down your new mental findings; you will be amazed at what comes up in the mind when you are on your own. **Solitude** is a blessing as it enables you to heal in a way that you would not be able to if you had people around you. It gently encourages you to be still with yourself. When you are still, then that is where the best thoughts enter the mind and intuition is heard more clearly. I believe this is one of the many reasons people meditate. For me, it is a must to spend quiet time in the morning, especially as that is when Intuition is heard at its loudest. I get my strongest ideas alone within the silence, and there is nothing wrong with shutting yourself away from the world while you either heal yourself or commit to looking inward to find yourself. A lot of truly successful people have done so and are reaping the benefits as a result of understanding the importance of silence. This is your life to do with as you please, and shutting everyone out for a while so as you can regroup your mind, body, and soul is a wise move, especially if you are looking for clarity, personal knowledge, your reason for being, or simply just want to shut the door and be alone with your own thoughts. Your real friends will respect your motives and happy for you.

"Come into the silence of Solitude and the vibration there will talk to you through the voice of God."

[Paramahansa Yogananda]

Exercise: Do what you can to avoid people for one month. If you are living in a space where you cannot avoid people, then the park, library, church, or wherever there is a quiet space where you can spend time for hours on your own is great. I used to go to my favourite book stores and sample all the self-help books while I was recovering. I found it helpful, informative, and it awakened new ideas in me, which were beneficial to my sobriety and wellbeing. If you happen to be fortunate enough to live on your own, then take this opportunity to let your friends know that you will be going into retreat for a month and would like not to be disturbed. The reason why I mention that you let people know of your plan is that they may start worrying about you if they do not see you, then someone is bound to come knocking on your door breaking your month's silence. Another reason is that once you have told them about your retreat, then should you last the whole month in solitude. The people you have told will most certainly see a positive difference in you, and when you see them, you will also notice a positive difference in yourself plus you will notice a difference in them too. In that month, you will make friends with Solitude, and if you are anything like me, you will possibly want to make future dates with your newfound friend. Of course, you may have to go to work, but sacrifice going out with your mates for a month or seeing anyone if that's possible. If you are a parent, you may have to adapt and find quite times for yourself by going to bed earlier and rising earlier so as you can have that quiet time to yourself before the household wakes up. I get up at 4:30 am every morning and my routine from then until 7:30 consists of shower, meditation, gym, writing in my latest book or a poem, then reading a chapter of a good book. I cram that all into 3 hours and that is my special time of the day earmarked for me and all done in silence. Put a date in your diary, discipline yourself and just go for it, you will be so pleased that you did.

SEEK

"There is no need to suffer in silence and there is no shame in seeking help."

[Joel S. Manuel]

SEEK advice from those who are now excelling in their life after having gone through what you already have, it is these people that you can learn from and get inspired by. If your poison was drugs, drink, sex addiction, gambling, being in an abusive relationship, or if you have suffered any other forms of abuse in the past, then seek out someone that has overcome that and is a success in their new chosen field. Seek out someone that has worked through that pain and is willing to share with you what they did to get to where they are today. Those who know, teach; and those who teach experientially are best placed to help you to evolve. We are all students of life, and many teachers can assist us with the knowledge we require to be the very best version of ourselves. A good teacher can assist us in getting to the next stage of our evolution, and there are many out there; when the student is ready, the teacher appears. "**What you seek is seeking you**" [**Rumi**]

Exercise:

1. Seek out ten people that have overcome a similar hardship to yours. It can either be someone you know locally or someone that you are inspired by online.
2. Take notes on each one of them and write down what you feel might be beneficial to your future wellbeing. If you find

yourself nodding in agreement with something that they did that you have not yet thought of, then write it down and make a plan to apply it in your life. If it has worked for them, then it can work for you also.

3. Always carry a pen and pad with you. Inspired ideas are like bubbles; they dissipate when your attention goes elsewhere. *"A short pencil is wiser than a long memory."* This is just one of the many ways you can elevate yourself to where you want to be.

SELF-HELP

"The spirit of Self-Help is the root of all genuine growth in the individual."

[Samuel Smiles]

"I was brought up by a parent that led me to believe that I had no value and it's human nature to destroy that which has no value. Thank God for self-help books that made me realise that I did indeed have value and that my life was actually worth more than the nothing I was initially encouraged to believe."
[Jennie Matthias]

SELF-HELP books that resonate with where you have been and where you see yourself in the future are a must, and if reading is not your thing, then there are also audio books that can be downloaded online. Friends of mine who are suffering from dyslexia prefer to listen to audios. Listening also has great benefits, for if you listen to something that resonates with you over and over again, it will soon sink into your psyche and go on to produce a nugget of wisdom whenever an opportunity arises that allows you to share when needed or apply to your life. It is a must that you pursue forms of Self-Help because you will discover that in doing so, you are NOT the only person that has gone through adversity. It softens the blow when you realise that you are in the company of others that truly understand; it could well be the catalyst for your full recovery. When you listen to another person's story, you are naturally compelled to take action within your own life, especially when people that have been through something similar are now making money and becoming successful by sharing their stories with the masses with a view to helping others. You can do that too; that could be you. Listening to a person's story that is similar to your own inspires you to kick your butt back into shape. It opens a mental channel that, in turn, fills the mind with positive messages on how to get back on track. When you look at the likes of Anthony Robbins, you see that this man took no prisoners when searching to help himself in areas that needed work within his life, and now look at this giant of a man, one of the most inspirational speakers of our time.

Self-help is everywhere nowadays, motivational speakers and self-help authors online are in many, from the likes of Tom Bilyeu, Anthony Robbins, Brian Tracy, Neville Goddard, Tim Rohn, Lisa Nichols, Robin Sharma, Oprah Winfrey, Les Brown, Wayne Dyer, Louise Hay, Martha Stewart, J.K. Rowling and the list goes on. When you step into this world, you open your mind to the positive, and when you are positive, you attract more of its kind. When you delve deeper, you experience a shift in vibration, and this offers you *solutions* to getting yourself back on track with the life you want to have and deserve. Try it for one month with no breaks and not only will you see what I mean, but you will never want to look back. You will acquire a thirst for more knowledge and there is nothing wrong with that, for this is how we grow.

EXERCISE: Start off looking online at any of the above speakers, even better if you do it in the month of solitude as this will be food for the mind and soul. Once you have looked and listened to all of them, you will no doubt be guided on to other great speakers, some that resonate with you even more. Find the ones that do it for you and keep playing them in the background, while you have a bath, do the dishes, or housework. I usually download the ones I like and then take them to the gym. It's usually the motivational speakers that get me all fired up to get to the gym, but listening to them does help, and more to the point charges me into action. After a morning or an afternoon of this, give yourself a break to soak it all in and then have some quiet time for yourself. Restart again the following morning or afternoon; eventually, these words of wisdom will remain in your psyche until you are able to use them at an opportune moment in time. If anything, listening to them constantly will change your perspective on life, yourself, and how you view others. Make a collection of these links to be tapped into at a click of a button, preferably on your iPod, travelling on the bus or tube is a great way to soak in the new information and will leave you with food for thought throughout the rest of the day and, of course, will positively inspire you. **"Ultimately, the greatest help is Self-Help." [Bruce Lee]**

SEARCH

"A man travels the world over in search of what he needs and returns home to find it."

[George A. Moore]

SEARCH for a mentor that understands your journey, someone with the knowledge to inspire you into action. Mentors or Role models are essential in your recovery and search for a better life. They can elevate you to a place of understanding, where you can grow to heights of your choosing. Mentors are a blessing to the universe, and it is my belief that they came to earth to endure hardship so that you don't have to - their mission is to use their experience to inspire those that have gone through a similar hardship and encourage them to take a better path than the one they once travelled. When you are truly ready, then chances are they may also search for you. It is a two-way thing helping each other and beneficial to you both. Deliberately go out to search for a better way of life in all things, health, wealth, wisdom, love and relationships, for anything less will possibly put you out of alignment and harmony with the planet and other people. Search for things that you like to do that make you happy and, as long as it is not harmful to another, then keep searching for more whilst showing gratitude for this new line of thought and way of being. **"He who would search for pearls must dive below" [John Dryden]**

EXERCISE: There are numerous people out there that have what you need to raise your vibration, but it's up to you to find them. When I was searching for ways to be inspired, I started off with books on how others had overcome adversity like Louise Hay's 'You Can Heal Your Life' - 'The Power Of Positive Thinking' By 'Norman Vincent Peale,' etc. What this did was to open my mind up to the possibility of being healed internally. My earlier years were fraught with violent parental behaviour towards me, and it had an adverse effect on my adult life. It was by choice that I would search out something better than what I had come to believe. Over the years, I have observed that when you decide to go down the avenue of searching for something better for yourself, then the universe hears your call and conspires to guide you to the right books, places, and people. It is a known fact that the Law Of Attraction works like this and it is a truth that many have also experienced as a manifestation of their thoughts. The old adage 'Ask and Ye Shall Receive' comes to play here, and it is highly relevant within this context as it really does work. There is a book by Neville Goddard called 'Feeling is The Secret' that explains how this works so much better than I do. As part of this exercise, please try and get yourself a copy, as there are only 47 pages to the book, each one offering nuggets of pure gold that, if applied to your life, will elevate you to the heights in which you seek to climb. Search for a mentor that understands your journey, one that has overcome all that you have been through and more, one that exudes health, wealth, wisdom, compassion, and has a strong desire to want to help you and others. There are many out there like myself that simply love it when they are given an opportunity to help. For the mentor, helping others is a way of justifying all that they have been through, for if they had not, then they would not be able to help you or anyone else. It makes all the past suffering so worth it, and in that way, they are happy to share their experiences with you with the aim of lifting your spirits, inspiring you to do the best for yourself. Make a point to ask your higher self for such a person to walk into your life or for you to walk into theirs. It will happen if you want it bad enough and I can tell you now that once you find the right one, your life will move at a faster pace and you will start to have more purpose in your life. A good mentor will help you to grow. You will also notice that your old ways of thinking will have many changes and those changes will be for the better. If you cannot find a person at first, then there are some excellent ones on YouTube who motivate, inspire, and share how they have overcome the difficulties they have endured on their journeys. Some of my favourites are Tom Bilyeu - Wayne Dyer - Lisa Nichols - etc. There are so many that you can instantly get inspired by while you are searching for one locally to you. You also might want to attend some seminars that speak about stuff that resonates with you. For me, I was very interested in what a guy called 'Andy Harrington' was offering at his 'Power To Achieve' seminar. It was a 4-day event, and it was also free or if you wanted to pay for Gold tickets, it was still less than £20.00, which I thought was a bargain, especially since I got to rub shoulders with people that were all wanting to do something positive with their lives but were at a crossroads just like me. I walked away elated and with a much better vision of not only what I wanted to do, but also where I wanted to go. From there on, I took one of their courses and have never looked back. I got involved in going to another event run by a lady called Michelle Watson, whose views on life resonated with me. Michelle kindly offered to be my mentor. I am now in a large group of like-minded people, all of which encourage each other with the progression of their projects and ideas. We now have a 'WhatsApp' group, and we give ourselves tasks and deadlines for doing the things we say we really want to do. Not only is it fun, but it's also a great way to ensure that we all build on our ideas and we share our progress regularly, which boosts the whole group and keeps us all active. Michelle is our mentor on there who offers us incredible guidance and shares healthy ideas that make our projects even more fruitful in areas we had not even thought of. So the exercise is to search for a mentor, get involved in attending a seminar or two that suits you, and then meet as many people that you can that have a similar interest to yours. Actively doing this means that you are showing the universe that you're ready. The universe, in turn, will see that and supply you with the information, environment, and whatever else is needed for you to meet the right mentor/teacher for you; when the student is ready, the teacher appears.

SUCCESS

"The best revenge is massive success."

[Frank Sinatra]

Success is for anyone who has a desire to be successful. If being successful is owning your own home or living the life of a pop-star, then there is no reason why you cannot have these things. If success is having a car, a new job, a new career, a marriage that works or whatever you see as a successful thing to have, then again there is no reason why you cannot obtain these things. To be successful, all you need to do is think it and believe in what it is you are thinking until you really feel it. Feeling successful is the secret to being successful. There is a fabulous book called 'Feeling is the Secret' by Neville Goddard, where it explains how to practice the art of feeling what it is you want to have in your life. It is so simple to grasp, yet many of us never seem to take notice of it possibly because it is so simple. When I was younger, I was called stupid, worthless, useless, and the list goes on. This did nothing for my self-esteem, and so my mindset was never one that promoted success because I was brought up to believe the opposite about myself, but my story took a strange twist when, by chance, I happened to be in the right place at the right time and was chosen by a studio producer who liked the sound of my speaking voice. He asked me while I was there to come in and sing the main part of a song that they had been recording. At the time, I didn't even know that I could sing, but they recorded me anyway and really loved my voice. Word soon got around, and then I was invited to audition with an all-girl band. I ended up getting the job as lead singer and the next thing you know, I am doing shows, signing record deals, playing Top of The Pops and travelling around the world living the pop star dream. I guess my mother was wrong about me being worthless then? I think other people at that time saw me as successful also. I totally get why a person would feel that being successful is not for them, but living a life defined by someone else's view of them is living a lie; think about it. Another thing about being successful is that more doors open for you and there seems to be a greater respect for you by others. Now that I am mentoring people that have gone through similar hardships as I did, I feel it is extremely important that I am seen as successful in my field for not only does it add weight to what it is that I do, but it also inspires the mentees into action when they see how someone like me can survive all they have been through and dare to be a success, no matter what was thrown my way. When my mentees see what I have done and still doing, they can see it as an achievable thing for them also. So I say strive to be successful, even if it's just a small area in your life where people can view that success. It could be that you have successfully mastered the art of going to the gym on a regular basis. You are a success in that area. You might want to go back to school and master a subject, strive to be a success in it. You may be a chef that cooks mouth-watering meals that people are ready to pay an arm and a leg for because you are so good at it, that's being a success, and the list goes on. Being successful at something is a feather in your cap, as you have a credential that can be used to either help, inspire, or make another person happy. When I go into any venture, I always strive to be successful at whatever it is I have gone into. **"Success just doesn't come out and find you, you have to go out and get it." [Anon]**

Exercise: There are numerous ways in which a person can be successful, and it does not have to be huge. Your exercise is to master one thing that you have always wanted to do. Start off with something small if the main thing you want to do is too large to accomplish at the moment, with a view to looking at the main thing and working out how you are going to get from A - Z to become a success. It is always a good idea to plan as success will not happen without movement. So make a plan, commit to adding something to helping you to achieve that plan every day. Right now, I am writing my first book, and I have committed myself to an hour in the morning, and one hour at night; that's two hours a day, fourteen hours a week, 56 hours a month and so on. The art is to keep moving toward your aim, mine is clearly to finish the book, and whether or not it is a bestseller, the fact will remain that I was successful in completing it. It's important for me to be a success in this area and so I adopt a strict, disciplined regime because I know that once I am finished, I will not only have added another feather to my cap, but I will also be able to share its contents with the world, and that will position me as an author. So your exercise can be anything you feel is important for you right now; it also has to be something that you have your heart set on, as if it is not, then you probably won't be successful in something your heart is not in tune with.

SELF-TALK

"Self-talk is the most powerful communication because it either empowers you or defeats you."

[Advanced Life Skills]

What we say to ourselves is one of the most important things we do for ourselves. Our self-talk can either make us or break us, it's a choice we have, it can uplift us up or bring us down and whichever one we choose determines our mood throughout the days, weeks, months, years, and a lifetime ahead. The subject of 'Self-Talk' and what it does to the mind, body, and soul should be taught in every school and added as a life topic to the curriculum. It always amazes me that children are taught things in school that they will never ever use in the outside world, yet it is my belief that if this simple metaphysical science was taught to everyone as soon as they were of an age of understanding, then people would flourish in so many positive ways and maybe much of the ills in our world would simply NOT exist.

When I say Self-Talk, what I mean is what we say to ourselves on a regular basis. You trip over a stone and you might say, I am so clumsy, I am so stupid, I am so such and such, or you might glance in the mirror and say something like, Ugh, I am getting old, I am losing my looks, I am ugly, etc. This is Self-Talk and it is usually so negative that it's a wonder that we get out of bed in the mornings. We are our own critics, no one criticises us more than we do and more often than not, we run this on a daily basis without batting an eye or even noticing that we do it. Let me tell you something;

this HAS to stop. You are damaging your energy and attracting more of what you think about. We are what we think all day long, and as such we make up our own reality with those thoughts. For years, I would look in the mirror and say I am ugly or I am average, and this would do nothing for my mood. How you talk to yourself determines how your day will become and how you see yourself is exactly how others will see you. It took me years and years to realise this, and now I do all that I can to stop myself in my tracks and look at me in a more positive light. Not only am I happier with life now, but all who know me have seen a huge change in my persona, and though they cannot put a finger on it, they clearly like the change. The right Self-Talk takes practice, so follow some simple exercises and make a go about changing your personal mindset for the better.

Exercise: Next time you stub your toe, trip up, say something you think was foolish, watch what Self-Talk follows. If the words, Oh, I'm such an idiot, I look awful today, I am too old for that etc. Come into play, then stop and immediately see it for what it is, A LIE. You are not an idiot, you don't look awful today, and you are NOT too old to do whatever it is. You are making all this up as you go along and it's silly. Try following the I AM with positive words like Beautiful, Happy, Loveable, Funny, Gentle, Loving, Caring, Kind, Wise, Healthy, Happy, Wealthy, etc. This exercise is to replace the old with the new. Meditate on the idea of changing your personal viewpoint, and you will experience an uplifting change, especially if you keep this up for at least a month. Doing an exercise like this every single day will eventually empower you and make you look at life more positively. Write down in your journal how many times you caught yourself and replace it with something more positive; eventually, you will finally stop mentally, beating yourself up.

STORY

"There is no greater agony than bearing an untold story inside you."

[Maya Angelou]

Every one of us has a story to tell; the longer you live, the bigger the story. What's your story going to be? Whose lives are you going to touch? Will your experience be a good one for you or your loved ones? Will you leave something behind that people will remember you for, or will you just fade away into the backdrop of time? Will anyone cry when you die, and if you had the chance to meet yourself on your death bed, would you be happy with what you have achieved or would you live life with sadness and regret? If you are still alive, then your stories are not over. You still have time to write and create the rest of your story; the choice is yours and the time is NOW.

The best illustration you can give someone is to use yourself and your experiences as an example to stress a point. Become a good storyteller. If you have been through something, then it's only you who can talk about it on a candid level and, as such, the people who listen are usually inspired by your story because it is obvious you have lived through it and are around to share that particular nugget of wisdom that may just save a person's life. Yes, people have the power to change a person's direction with the power of words, stories, and anecdotes. History is littered with success stories on how people inspire others through their true life experiences. Some have gone as far as to even write their full life's experience using poetry as a tool to get their story out there. Everyone has a story to tell, but not everyone is brave enough to tell it.

EXERCISE: Get a book that allows you to write at least 50 pages (25 pages for the past and 25 pages for the future or how you wish to see it), and start your story from as far back as you can remember. Write down the most significant, good, or bad moments. The ones that come to mind first, go through each one until the present day and then look back at each one, building on one category at a time, you will find that as you focus on one, then many other memories flood back. The idea behind this exercise is not to write a book (although the content you come up with could be used as an autobiography), rather it is for you to write as much as you can from what you know using the first 25 pages. The next 25 pages are going to be how you see yourself in the future until the end. It does not matter if you believe what you are writing when creating a story for your future you, it only matters that it is beneficial to your wellbeing and you are happy with how your future self is turning out. Who are you going to be? Who are you going to help? Where are you going to live? What sort of house are you living in? Do you have a well-paid job or are others working for you? Can your past experiences be brought into your future as a way of assisting humanity? This exercise is about looking back and looking forward, stretching the imagination and making you think about how far you have come and how much further you are willing to go to realise your dreams. The exercise is not done until the 50 pages are full. Once you have filled up all the pages, the action of writing down past and future will inspire you into action in some way or another. Another exercise would be to search for a local storytelling group that will give you honest feedback about your approach to storytelling. It is a way of improving your communication skills. Practice makes perfect, and a truly good story coupled with an impenetrable approach will position you as an expert in your chosen field. For me, my next incarnation will be as a public speaker, and even though I know I am a good storyteller, I am always looking for ways to improve my approach and by actively going out there to check out what's currently on offer, I soak in my findings and enhance my own unique qualities further. I like being original, and I make a point of going out and checking the terrain to see if anyone is doing it better than me. And if they are, it then inspires me to re-think my approach and delve deeper into myself for that extra special something that makes my storytelling an incredible experience for the listener. Work on becoming a GREAT storyteller, and you will gain the ear of the people that will assist you in your growth. **"Stories of imagination, tend to upset those without one."** [**Terry Pratchett**]

STAGE

All the world's a stage, and all the men and women merely players: they have their exits and their entrances; and one man in his time plays many parts, his acts being seven ages."

[William Shakespeare]

The world is a stage, and its people are actors playing parts of their choosing. Some choose bit parts while others go the full hog for recognition. Then there are others that prefer to work behind the scenes, happy to assist with making it all happen. Any bit part player could play a more prominent role, it's just a matter of choice. Where we are today is all down to the choices we make, and we act out every role we choose for which there are many. With this in mind, I am curious to know where exactly you see yourself on the world stage? What part are you playing at the moment? What part would you like to play? Remember, you have the choice to be anyone you want to be. Are you a hero, A Lover, an Angel, a Matchmaker, a President, a Philanthropist, an Award-Winning Author, a Successful Celebrity figure, Teacher, Nurse, Footballer, Public Speaker, Police Officer, Stock Broker, Model, Sports Personality, Fireman, Pop-star, Artist, Poet, Songwriter, Mother, Father, Dustman, Road Sweeper, Hairdresser, Toilet Attendant, Banker, Traffic Warden, Spiritual Healer, Guru, Cleaner, Drug Addict, Alcoholic, Fugitive, Criminal, Judge, Prisoner, Soldier, the choice is endless on roles to pick, which one are you? Which one would you like to be? In life, we have worn many hats, which means we have played many roles, and the longer we live, the more roles we are required to play, but the choice of role is always ours. Below is a picture of me performing in front of a large audience. I went from wearing the hat of being very shy and afraid to speak up to commanding an audience. The choice was mine, and I took it. I practice this throughout my whole life now.

EXERCISE: You will need your pen and pad for this. Recall how many roles you have played from the past to current date and how each one made you feel? That is, were you a prefect in school? Were you a factory worker, checkout staff, etc. All these are roles, and all roles you play have feelings and emotions attached to them. How did you feel in those roles and are you still in them? When you look at all the roles you have played, you will notice that each one has brought you to where you are today. There will be a thread running through each thing that you have done. For me, I started out in life as a neglected, rejected, and abused child. This experience took time to shake off and so for a while, I wore the hat of a victim of life. I then associated myself with the drug world and wore the hat of a drug addict. I eventually threw that hat away and decided to teach what I knew about those drug experiences and wore the hat of a creative teacher going into schools creating Drug Awareness projects for children. In between that time, I also managed to wear the hat of a Famous Pop-star, Model, Public Speaker and Charity worker, I am sure I have worn many more, but the moral of my sharing this is that each thing I did brought me closer to my Life's Purpose. Without the experience of wearing all those hats, I would not have found it. When you take a deeper look into what you have done in the past, it makes you think about where you are now and where you might like to see yourself in the future. The older you get, the larger the toolbox of experience you acquire and, as such, you are in the most powerful position to become a teacher, speaker, and leader in your field, which means you will no doubt be seen in another hat. What hat can you see yourself wearing in the future? Will the hat you wear next be associated with your reason for being, and will it help you to gain access into knowing and understanding your Life's Purpose? Once you do an exercise like this, it will make you think and will most certainly inspire some fresh ideas that you will be able to apply to something positive in your future.

CHAPTER 3

UNDERSTANDING SELF

"I understood myself only after I destroyed myself, and only in the process of fixing myself, did I know who I really was."

[Sade Andria Zabala]

I would certainly agree with the quote above having gone through many years of not understanding or indeed knowing myself. After my self-destruction, it took time for me to repair and while I was on that journey to healing myself, I discovered things about me that I had never known before. Often times we can just go through life being lost souls, not realising that we are lost until something like a tragedy either shakes us to our core, or we come so close to death before we finally wake up. In order for others to understand you, you really have to understand yourself. Throughout life, we go through many stages of thinking we know what we are only to reinvent ourselves into the next thing that we think we are. We are our family, we are our environment, we are our community, we are our image, we are our etc., but all these things that we have picked for ourselves are outside of us and seldom have we ventured inside to really discover our true self. Eastern philosophies encourage us to look within when meditating and many successful people have adopted the art of meditation prior to each working day. There is something in this for sure as many more people are becoming aware of the benefits of this simple philosophy. Meditation enables you to open your mind, and in doing so, you acquire a better understanding of your mind, body, and soul. The world within is so much more than the outside world. I find that when I ask a question maybe the night before, an answer appears in my quiet time of morning meditations. Sometimes I can almost hear my intuition guiding me to specific solutions that I have been trying to work out, and when it comes to understanding myself, meditation has played a huge role.

EXERCISE: Meditate for 15 minutes, preferably first thing in the morning before eating and progress into an evening session for the same amount of time before going to sleep. If you are unsure of how to meditate, then find someone that can show you or look at some of the teachers on YouTube. Also, there are many places that teach free meditation locally. Meditation is not as easy as it looks, so this is a big exercise and will require a lot of patience from yourself and your mind. Like me, you might possibly get frustrated at first as the mind is usually all over the place, but the task is to learn how to calm the mind and so patience is a must. Even the most revered teachers of meditation had to start somewhere, and they all experienced the same thing. It takes time, but when you start to get it, you are on your journey to understanding self. Meditation is about looking within, and once you discover the benefits of this Eastern practice, you will not look back. You will also be able to apply it to different aspects of your life when certain answers are being sought. I find myself meditating on the question, then soon after, I am guided to find the answer. Learning how to meditate is one of the most important things you do for yourself.

UNIQUE

"Embrace your Uniqueness, time is much too short to be living someone else's life"

[Kobi Yamada]

Being Unique is your birth right; it is your personal stamp of oneness. There was and never will be anyone like you on this planet. No one will ever have the same fingerprint as you and no one will ever have exactly the same experiences as you. They may have something similar, but it will NEVER EVER be the same as you because they are **<u>NOT</u>** you. You are the one and only you, and although people may copy you for whatever reason, they can *never ever* be you. Once you grasp this, you will start to recognise your worth. It is true of not only you, but every being on earth; however, many go to their graves not realising their greatness because they were too afraid to show off their unique qualities for fear of ridicule, or maybe along their journey, they might have acquired the heavy load of low self-esteem that made them shy away from life-changing opportunities. There is nothing wrong with being different, but there is everything wrong in not embracing what you are. You were born Unique for a reason, so don't be selfish. Let your Uniqueness shine so as we can bask in its rays and learn from your beautiful being, from your awesomeness, for you are truly unique.

EXERCISE: You will also need a pen and pad for this one: Look in the mirror and ask yourself what you have that is different from others. Look at yourself very deeply, and I guarantee something will come up that will prompt you to take some notes... write down 10 things that you feel make you different from your peers or other people. It could be the way you look at things, the way you like to dress, your attitude, your outspoken but honest manner, whatever that is, write it down and once you have found those things, make a point of embracing them and sharing them with others. The idea is NOT to tone down your Uniqueness, but to develop it further because it is that which makes you stand out. Look at where your Uniqueness might be of benefit to yourself and others, place it in a situation and environment where it will be appreciated. For instance, I have a Unique quality when it comes to being creative with words, and so I create poetry and am able to memorise and position myself in places that would appreciate hearing those words. I LOVE writing, and so it's really easy for me to write, but I am also a very brave performer, and I perform what I create. No one is able to perform the thing that I created in the way in which I did it, as I wrote it, and since it came from within me, I am the master at approaching how to perform that content in a way that will make others sit up and take notice. My approach is Unique. I would say to you that you certainly have a Uniqueness about you. If you cannot see it, then ask some of your friends if they think there is anything Unique about you, and if so, can they tell you what it is as you are doing an exercise? **"Do not underestimate yourself by comparing yourself with others. It's our differences that make us unique and beautiful"**

UPGRADE

"Don't downgrade your dreams to match your reality, upgrade your faith to match your destiny."

[Anonymous]

If your thoughts are always negative about you, your situation, or others, then it's time for an upgrade as negative thoughts are like a virus in the computer of your mind. Every time you are on a negative about you, your friends, neighbours, family or strangers, you are collecting viruses, which affect the workings of your mind computer. In this case, your mind, body, and soul are being infected with a virus that will eventually affect the functioning of your thoughts causing stress, sleeplessness, worry, and more negativity. When you think dark thoughts, you also attract them, and there is little room for light to come in when you are in that mode of thinking. People usually avoid those who are constantly allowing themselves to be infected with bad viruses as they are aware that sort of disease is highly contagious and brings the vibration down to the level of the infected person. The cure for this is to watch your thoughts and actions like a hawk and slowly change your attitude towards yourself and others, to see things in the opposite, from bad to good, dark to light, negative to positive. After a few months or deliberately choosing a better choice of data, you will notice that your personal computer [which is your mind] will run so much smoother than it ever did before because you made the choice to upgrade your thoughts. Your energy will be running at a higher vibration and, therefore, you will be attracting people that have a more positive outlook in life. Your conversations with others will be different, and you will have more friends because people love being around positive people and you will feel much lighter not to mention sleep better at night. Upgrading you is one of the most important things that you do with yourself for the rest of your life. It's you being your greatest teacher and taking charge of how you are and want to be seen as a person. Most people on this planet yearn to be liked or loved and keeping an eye out for those viruses with a view to upgrading every time you notice a glitch is imperative if you want to be your greatest self ever.

EXERCISE: Write down 10 or more thoughts about how you honestly see yourself. It does not matter if what you write is negative, as this is the exercise. Look closely at each thing that you have written and then write its positive opposite. If it is already positive, then leave it that way or add something else positive beside it. This is an exercise in upgrading your thoughts, and when you write something down, it usually encourages you to think about it on a deeper level. It's best to do these exercises with a pen and paper, before adding anything to the computer. When you write on paper, it is an organic feeling, from thought to paper. To write a series of letters is different from tapping the keys and requires a different more memorable movement and experience.

USEFULNESS

"The true happiness of a man is having a clear conscience and being useful for humanity."

[Tolstoy]

We are not here on this plane just to serve ourselves; we are here to be of service to others also. Everyone has something that is useful to another, whether it be passing on knowledge gained through experience, being able to step into a situation where you know that your help would be immeasurable to a person or group of people. I remember when I decided to come off of drugs, I went out seeking volunteer work so as I could keep my mind off of things and do something different that would deter me from going back down that path. I was unsure of what would be required of me, but I felt that as a person willing to offer up their time for a worthy cause, there would be something that I had that might be useful to them. I was prepared to do the most menial of tasks from folding up leaflets to making the tea all of which are useful in certain situations. It so happened that I could type really fast, I have a good command of English, and I am a great songwriter. I am also highly creative, and I was driven by my selfish mission to stay clean. I joined a Women's group who were helping survivors of unimaginable torture to cope with their pain and assist them with their rights. My reason for being there in the first place soon got forgotten about when I realised that there were people out there in pain brought on by circumstances out of their control and not of their own doing. This made me realise two things. 1) that I had been highly selfish abusing myself in the way that I had done for years, and 2) that I had the tools to be of some positive use to this hardworking group of people doing all they could to make the lives of these women manageable. It's a strange thing; when you see others in trouble, all you want to do is help, and you just do it, because you know you can, and what's more, you really want to be of some use to those who would appreciate what you could do for them. Every single person on this planet has a use for someone, and it is the most healing of acts when you put your mind to helping others. Being useful in another person's life is so very important to them, but in addition, it also plays a positive part in raising your self-worth. All of a sudden, you will be around people that value you as a person, and feeling valued is a truly wonderful feeling. It elevates your mood and raises your vibration. This feeling promotes a sense of wanting to do even more and finding new ways on how your usefulness can be extended to assist an even wider audience. Being useful to others is one of the most beneficial things you can do to raise your self-esteem as it is an act of sheer LOVE. "**Love comes into being through useful service to others.**" [**Emmanuel Swedenborg**]

Exercise: Every day for 7 days, or even better for one month, go out and search for areas where you can be of assistance, even if it is just opening the door for a person struggling to get in with their baggage, walking a senior citizen across the road, helping a lady with a pram up the escalators, making the tea at a volunteers group one day a week, joining a local group of people intending on helping those less fortunate than themselves, visit a hospital and see if there is a place where you might be able to be a friend to a lonely dying person, do the neighbours shopping, the list of things you can do to assist others with being useful is endless. This exercise is to do at least one thing every single day. When you get back home, then write about the situation, how it made you feel to be in the right place at the right time to be of use, what it was that you did that was so useful and even what the response was when you offered your help. Once you look at your weekly or monthly list, you will note the following things. A) You did something useful and made a person's life a little bit better, B) You rose to the challenge, and in doing so, you recognised that you do have some worth, C) you feel that tad more significant in the scheme of things. It's a great exercise and one that I do daily. When I am on the underground, there have been many opportunities for me to help someone up or down the stairs with a heavy suitcase. It takes a few moments, and the relief that it gives that person is immense. If you have the power to be useful in that way, then share it, it is a gift that has been given to you to do so.

UNTOUCHABLE

"Stay wise and the mind is untouchable."

[Rakim]

Untouchable, lying beyond reach, unable to be touched by anything else in its field. Be Untouchable in whatever it is you endeavour to do, and by that, I mean indestructible. I have a knack at being able to write about things I observe in a poetic way that gets the ear of many people, and in this way, I am Untouchable as my approach to the content I share with a wide audience is done with an unshakable style. No other artist can touch my personal approach with the content I created, as it came from me and so only I can share it from a deeper level as it is part of me. It came from my being, my heart, my observations, and coupled with a style perfected over many years, it is this that makes each sketch I create untouchable. Cassius Clay, Bruce Lee, and many others have mastered their craft over so many years to the point where they were UNTOUCHABLE. Connor McGregor and many sports people have that ability along with some of the most incredible names throughout our existence on this planet that have given their lives to save others. They are UNTOUCHABLE in their field. Do you have anything that you feel that you would like to do with your life and become so masterful and solid at it that NO ONE could touch you?

Exercise: Look for the one thing that you feel that you would like to be a master at and write down 5 - 10 ways in which you can start to make that happen and what it will take for you to become 100% UNTOUCHABLE in your chosen field. Also, write down the things that are stopping you from doing what you would like to do. Look back at what you have written and make a point of slowly taking out of your life those things which no longer serve your purpose of self-mastery. This exercise will make you think about where you are at right now in your life and who you are willing to leave behind to get to your goal. In life, there are always going to be people that hold you back from being a master in your field. It's OK to slowly distance yourself from them, especially when it's done with LOVE. Be a master in your field, be UNTOUCHABLE!

UPLIFT

"We rise by lifting others."

[Robert Ingersoll]

Within this category, it is very important for you to do whatever you can to uplift your spirits and then go on to uplift others. It is part of your growth and beneficial to everyone. When you walk into a room of moody people, that rubs off on you in no time, but if a person who is moody and negative walks into a room where everyone is uplifted in spirit, they cannot help but walk away with a positive boost. Every person on this planet has the ability to raise a person's spirit. Offer them hope, throw them a smile, and encourage them to see themselves in a positive light. Everyone has that power, yet few realise the power a simple, uplifting gesture can do for someone else. I make it my life's work to uplift the lives of those I come in contact with as I recognise the power that simple action has for them and then myself. If you had the power to change the world for the better, would you sit there and not bother or would you get to work and do what was required? Well, you do have the power to change another person's world, and since you are still alive, then you have the tools to be a master in this area. On a personal level, it is important that you search for ways in which to uplift your own spirit because when you lift yourself up, you are in a better position to lift up others. I read inspirational quotes and pass them to literally thousands of people on the internet. I have a huge following, and so I choose one of the best I can find for that day, title it 'QUOTE OF THE DAY.' It usually gets quite a few hundred hits and many comments on how that quote came at exactly the right time. That gesture enabled me to uplift many people in one hit. I also make a point of saying good morning to strangers in the street, followed by a cheerful smile. The look on their face says it all; they always smile back and if it was the only time they smiled throughout that day, then cool, at least for one moment in time they were smiling. Surround yourself with things that uplift your soul; it could be books, flowers, clean apartment, nice people, walking in the park, on the beach, having a sauna, going to the gym, whatever floats your boat, do it for you and strive to be happy.

EXERCISE: Look for ways in which you can uplift a person today and the rest of the week who you think could use it. Remember, it might just be as simple as a smile or kind words; you might act upon something that can help a person, which, in turn, will uplift them. Start with two a day and progress onto many more; this is a lifelong exercise. "**Look for a way to lift someone up, and if that's all you do, then that's enough.**" **[Elizabeth Lesser]**

CHAPTER 4

REPROGRAMME

"Programming your mind with positive thoughts each day will go a long way to keep you from allowing external criticism to derail your dreams."

[Ken Poirot]

If like me, you were programmed to believe in a lie about your ability to be anything other than what one person viewed you as, then it's time for you to stop. Look at that past programming and reprogramme your mind with more positive thoughts. In my case and at an early age, I was taught to believe what my Mother thought of me. The words stupid, ugly, useless, ridiculous, no one is going to listen to you, would grace my ears on a daily basis coupled with such venom that it would have a lasting effect on my later life. That sort of programming became a huge hindrance to me when it came to me believing in myself, the aftermath of which caused me to have severe low self-esteem. Eventually, I found myself drawn to spending time with people whose view on me were the total opposite of my Mother's, and my love of books and thirst for knowledge soon saw me reading and listening to self-help books. The new friends would advise me to read some book or other that would then go on to elevate my mind and help to dissolve my past programming. It was the best thing I could have done at that time, for if I had not done so, I would still be stuck in a dark place confused about life and my next steps within the great scheme of it all. Reprogramming my mind with new ideas and new reasons for being were something I practised every day as I just felt that what I was being guided toward spoke to me on such a deep level that I was compelled to look further into my reason for being and everybody else's. After quite a while, I began to start realising that I actually did have some worth and all the things that I was told in the past were actually one person's opinion of me, and everyone that I met after that sort of parenting were all saying the complete opposite. When you make a choice to reprogramme your mind, you make a conscious decision to clean up your head and line of thinking, much in the same way you would look at your apartment and decide that the old furniture is now in need of renewing. You make plans to get rid of it and replace it with the new, and when you do that, you feel refreshed, happy with your surroundings, and everything has a certain wellbeing feeling about it. The decision to look at your current thoughts and say to yourself that you are no longer going to think like this is just you wanting to replace the old furniture that no longer serves you with the new that will freshen your environment. I have come across many people, including myself, who have started their lives with dysfunctional and often times violent parents and siblings, which can make one become quite negative, but it does not have to be that way. I know many that have gone down the path of drink and drugs to quell the pain or escape what has now become demons in their head. They found that drink or drugs or promiscuous sex or even working themselves to the grave would fill a void where not much else had been able to touch before. But as we know with all the above that it is short-lived, a temporary crutch and does not deal with the reality of life and will just send us further into the abyss, so reprogramming the mind is a must for those wishing to seek positive change within their lives. If I had my way, I would most certainly add this to the school curriculum.

Exercise: Look at any friends or so-called family and friends you have and ask yourself, do their words about you resonate with you in a positive way? If they do not, then maybe it might be an idea to start finding new friends, and although it is said that you cannot change your family, you can most certainly find new families to adopt you or even you adopt them as a parent. My little sister did this, she actively went out to find parents that might love her, and it positively changed her life for the better.

- ✓ Find more positive people to spend your time with
- ✓ Look for audio or reading books that may transform your thinking
- ✓ Meditate with groups or join a yoga class, or do both
- ✓ Go to seminars where the people who attend are seeking positive change
- ✓ Be around people whose aims are to inspire others as well as themselves

REFORM

"A man that has reformed himself will reform thousands."

[Yogananda]

When a person reforms themselves, they usually have the respect of all those that have witnessed that reformation. I remember a time where people saw me as a lost cause until one day they noticed me getting a lot of coverage in the local papers, back on the music scene, and in-between that doing my bit for charity. I never announced that I was going to reform myself. I just did it, and the rest spoke for itself. In turn, that act re-opened many doors for me as I soon became a person of positive interest and one worth knowing, for I now had the tools to assist those who were struggling to cope through adversity much in the same way that I had done and used those tools. When you become a reformed person, especially when people have all but given up on you, then your life changes usually for the better. In order for you to get to the next stage in your journey, you must reform your way of thinking, being and even looking. To reform is to totally change, the way you once were, and in doing so, you change the thoughts of others around you. To reform is a positive thing to do for yourself as that particular part of your journey enables you to observe human nature in a way that you had possibly not seen before. You will always get the non-believers who will then end up eating their words once you have reformed.

Deep within you, you know what sort of person you want to be. When I was on drugs and couldn't see a way out. When I finally found a way out, I then dedicated all my time to coming off. It was a hard road, but I did it and am here to tell the tale. The change in me was remarkable, but I did not stop there. I chose to use my experience of being a user of class 'A' drugs to teaching school children and adults about the prevention of drugs and the effects they would have if they were taken. In that way, I was a reformed character and went on to do so much more in that area for quite a few years, which got people's interest and established me as a person in the know. Those who know, teach. I had gone from drug addict to accomplished teacher, that's what I mean about reform; unequivocal change. "**Self-reform automatically brings about social reform.**" [**Ramana Maharshi**]

EXERCISE: Look at your past experiences and what knowledge you have collected from them. Ask yourself if that knowledge can positively assist another person or organisation? Chances are you will have certain wisdom through your experiences that others could use. Do what you can to place yourself in a position in which to assist those with interest in knowing what you know. You may be surprised what you can do for others with your knowledge. Become a volunteer in a place that would relish what you know, even if it's for one day a week or month; this is a healthy exercise that you will greatly benefit from.

RISK

"He who is not courageous enough to take risks will accomplish nothing in life."

[Muhammad Ali]

There was a time that I was too scared to take a risk, as my self-esteem was so low that I feared doing anything that might elevate me in any way. I always assumed that I would probably not be that good at it, or good enough, but that was then, and this is now and my years have seen this meek, shy, fearful girl go from cowering in corners and hiding behind excuses to performing on stage in front of thousands of people and some. As the lead singer of a famous pop group, I would be seen in everyone's living room, as we were regulars on Top Of The Pops, which was the largest TV music show in the UK. If I hadn't taken a risk, I would still be afraid of my own shadow let alone be able to perform in front of thousands of people. I can honestly say that taking risks in life are one of the most essential tools for personal growth. It matters not if the risk you take is a failure, as each time you fail is a lesson learnt and offers you the insight on how you can do better next time. It's about the journey, it then becomes a game until the risk you take grows fruit. These days, taking risks are not just fun, but are an essential part of my growth. Taking risks have found a positive place within my daily routines from going to the gym to creating a new poem, writing a new song, or simply going for something really new and out of my comfort zone. My personal motto on risks is "If you don't try, you won't fly." If you are a person that likes to write poetry but has never performed it, then hang around those that do. There are many places that have open mic sessions, and trust me, there are people in there going on stage for the first time taking risks, and the feeling they get after having done that is liberating for them. It also becomes quite addictive, especially if people like what you have to say; I would call that a successful risk. I was at a Survivors poetry club not long ago, and it was for people that had come out of the mental health system and felt they had something to say and so they found ways of expressing themselves through writing and then performing. For most of them, it was a risk, but they were among like-minded people, all of which had taken a risk to air their poetry or songs in front of that audience. Some of them have gone on to do great things with their works and even have their own books out now, none of which would have happened if they had not taken a risk. If poetry or performing in front of an audience is not your thing, then there may be another area in your life that requires you to take a risk. Standing up for myself was a risk I was prepared to take after years of abuse, and although it was shaky for me at first, it gave the person who had been verbally abusive towards me a shock and also changed their behaviour towards me; wish I'd done it years ago.

EXERCISE: Simply do four things in one month that you have always wanted to do but have been too afraid to or thought that you were not capable of. Take the risk and do it anyway. You MUST do one a week and complete it, and then afterwards document the experience and emotions you had after completing it. Let's say, if it was to overcome heights and the risk was you taking the opportunity to go up in a hot air balloon, for instance, I would imagine that you might have something to say about it. Write down those experiences as when you do that, you will observe something about yourself that you had never done before. Only when you jump off the cliff will you be able to truly fly; be brave and take a risk.

RELATIONSHIPS

"The wrong relationships teach you how to recognise the right one when it arrives."

[Anonymous]

Relationships are all important to your personal growth as they can make or break your spirit. Over the many years I have been on this earth, I have experienced both good and bad, but all have helped me to understand the human experience and all have shaped my life in some way or another. I feel blessed at the number of friendships and relationships I have had already throughout this lifetime, and although quite a few did not make the grade to be with me in my later years, I am still appreciative of their existence in my life at one point. My feelings act as a radar for unwanted relationships. If I feel drained or exhausted, I avoid; if I feel uplifted and happy, I stay put. I am at an age where I now choose my friends wisely. Due to my vast experiences with them, I have become more philosophical about where I would like to go with future relationships and friendships. I recognise that to walk my chosen path will also require relationships that are encouraging, respectful, caring, understanding, inspiring, positive, protective, reassuring, friendly, honest, loving, kind, helpful, empathic, supportive, collaborative, and generous. I have always made a lot of headway when being involved with people that have these qualities, and it is these sort of people that I prefer to spend most of my time with in my later years. Recently, I went to a seminar that happened to be filled with like-minded people. All wanting to do something for themselves and their communities, we spent four days at this event. The tea and lunch breaks gave us an opportunity to get to know each other as did the group sessions we were encouraged to form within the seminar itself. We all got something so fabulous out of the four days that when the time came to say goodbye, it was actually quite emotional for many of us and so someone had the great idea of creating a 'WhatsApp' group for us all to stay in touch, inspire, and empower each other regularly. This group is still going, and there have been many successes as a result of the on-going support of the group. We are a creative, motivational, caring team who wants the best for each other and it can only be described as a beautiful thing. I, along with others in the group, have shared our new ideas to be critiqued by the group before airing it out in public. What you have here when you do that is a group of people who can add an idea that might enhance your work further. This is a great example of picking the right people to assist you in your growth. As people, we are always growing, but it's our relationships with others that can boost that growth. I have also been in bad relationships where my mood was always down and my whole being unhappy. When you are unhappy in this way, it stuns you spiritually and mentally. It's like walking on thick softened tar; you want to get to a place, but you are slowed down by each movement you take in the tar. Some people are scared to leave what they know and would rather have a lot of those they call friends than just a few that could be so much more beneficial to their well-being. To them, I would say, "You'll learn."

Eventually, you move away from the sort of people that put you down, beat you up, abuse you, threaten you, make your life a misery, emotionally blackmail you, and the list of nastiness goes on. Everyone has the right to choose who they wish to spend time with. No one has to be in an abusive relationship, especially these days where there is so much awareness of how very wrong it is to be in one, and especially if there are children involved. I could write a whole book on this subject alone, but will leave it up to your gut to make the choice because it is literally about how a person makes you feel. Feeling is your radar; when in doubt, leave it out. If the man in your life doesn't make you feel amazing, then maybe he's not the right man for you and vice versa? Is someone you call a friend always putting you down or making you feel uncomfortable? Are you afraid of being friends with someone but remain to be friends with them anyway for reasons you cannot fathom? Do you worry what a person you know is saying about you behind your back? All of those are negatives, and you will know how each one makes you feel when you just bring up their names. A good relationship makes you feel fabulous, and a bad one doesn't. It's all about how you would prefer to feel; you do have a choice, make yours wisely. **"Treasure your relationships, not your possessions." [Anthony J D'Angelo]**

EXERCISE: For this, you will need your pen and pad again, plus a sense of honesty. Write a list of all the traits you like about the people you are currently hanging about with. Choose the ones you like the most first and then progress onto incidental friends, then write about how each one of those people makes you feel. If you have a lot of people you call friends, then this may take some time, but it is essential that you write them all down. This can also include your family members. Next stage is to honestly ask yourself how your life would be without certain ones in your life. Again, be honest here and don't be afraid to write about family if they are the ones that you feel are stunting your growth or indeed making you happy or unhappy. Once you have done all of that, look at the list and ask yourself who you would miss if they were no longer in your life. This exercise is about making you think about how many people you can actually call your friend or good family member. Look at the lists again and make your choice; it sounds harsh, but you only have one go at this particular life on earth, so why wouldn't you make it one that is beneficial to your well-being? Once you give yourself a chance to view what it is that you truly have, you will see yourself slowly distancing from those that you choose not to spend any more time with. It really is okay to move on.

ROLE MODEL

You can either have one or be one; either way, the idea of a Role Model/Mentor is all positive. On a personal level, I know that if I had not had one or two show up in my life, then it is likely I might not have lived as long as I have. Role models are people that I shall always respect, remember, and love; anything I do now is because of them, and it is my duty not to let their words of love and the patience they had with me fade away. I always hoped to be a role model for someone one day in the hope that I too could pass the baton on to someone that may benefit from the knowledge I have gained over the years. I am happy to say that my hopes in that area have since been fulfilled, there is one lady in particular that I was given the opportunity to mentor, who speaks on this subject so very well. Her name is Shauna O'Briain, and her early years were fraught with much anguish, fear, and loathing. I totally understood Shauna's pain and frustration as it seemed we had almost parallel lives and so it was easy to offer guidance. Shauna has since used her experiences to help others who have gone through similar hardships. In doing so, she has helped thousands of young people to find their voice, speak up about their experiences in a creative manner, and provided a platform for them to expand on their creative skills of expressing themselves. By sharing her survival techniques with young people, Shauna has taken the baton I passed on to her and used it in the most powerful of ways. Shauna has now become the Role Model. Coupled with the gift of creativity, Shauna uses poetry as a tool to educate the masses on a deep soul level. Many of Shauna's experiences can be found within her poetic performances, and as such she has managed to gain the respect of not only people that are going through personal pains brought on by abusive upbringings, but Shauna has also captured the hearts of those in power that have positioned her in a place where she can get her message out there to a wider audience. Shauna was the founder of 'Lyrically Challenged,' the most revered Urban Hip Hop Poetry night in the UK and given that she is also dyslexic, she in no way let that stop her from teaching others how to express their inner feelings. Shauna has gone on to do educational programmes on TV, teach in various schools and clubs, created her own projects and pitched successfully for funds that would enable many others to attend those youth projects. Shauna now has a book out called 'MOMENTS OF SIGNIFICANCE,' which is a great read for anyone trying to get to grips with a neglectful upbringing. With Shauna's full permission, I share with you all a poem she wrote about the subject of being a ROLE MODEL.

"The role model in my home
Was carved into beer cans and needles
Heroes on my end are rated for a time in the pen
I'm not talking 'bout writing'
Getting locked up is normal
Role models are criminals
Carving an existence
From an environment of poverty
All I saw were victims of the system
At night, I would envision a different way of living
Bright lights, I'm an actress, a star
Reality was my estate trapped behind bars
I didn't know how to become a woman
The women around me were filled with pollution
Lost in a storm of confusion

My hostel full of drug abuse
I found Jen, my mentor, and she provided me with armour
She was the first women I had met that was a survivor
I was searching for a woman to show me how to live
How to create a positive life
A role model
To make it real
Cause I knew I had potential
How can you change if you don't have any examples
I modelled a new shape
With the wisdom
I can create
I have the power, thus is how dreams are made
My Gratitude exudes
I'm now a survivor
My battle scars to prove
The hell I walked through
Now I am a role model for the youth
A living example that you can make it two
Kids aren't born killers
Yet the hood life is claiming victims
Blood-stained pavements
Cause violence creates status
Role models are the G's on the block
Need more positive men on the block
Need mentors to role model new behaviour for the murders to stop
Life isn't just receiving; it's giving
Supporting each other to manifest our visions
We're just asked to live as the best we can be
Cause my victory is your victory

And your victory is mine
Forever connected
Build the world we would like to see
The Role Model
Makes it possible
Shows us the road."

EXERCISE: Role Models and Mentors are equipped with knowledge gained through personal experience and so are more than capable to teach on an experiential level. I assume that if you are reading this book, then you might be someone that has possibly lived through some harsh times where throughout, you will certainly have obtained numerous experiences most of which place you in a powerful position to help others who may be struggling to cope through adversity. Your exercise is to write or record as many experiences that you have endured both good and bad, express yourself on how each one made you feel and how you are coping with the not so pleasant ones. When we go back into our past with a view to helping others, we find the whole experience quite cathartic, and it does two things; it heals us so as we can heal others. Be the role model that you wish you had or you have experienced in someone that has inspired you. What you know you can teach, and you could possibly save a person's life by doing so. Be a role model for someone that is struggling to go through what you have come out of the other side from.

RESPECT

"Respect yourself enough to walk away from anything that no longer serves you, grows you, or makes you happy."

[Anonymous]

If you have no respect for yourself, then how can you expect others to have or treat you with respect? Respect then starts with you. When you look in the mirror, can you honestly say, RESPECT? Or are there doubts about that? Do you have respect for the way you look, what you do, or what you have become? I remember a time when I was so lost and ravished by drugs that I didn't even want to see my reflection in the mirror. I didn't like what I had become and, therefore, lacked any form of self-respect. While I was like this, I would hide myself away so as those friends of the past would not see what I had turned into. I wanted to avoid their reaction to what I had done to myself.

It is a human characteristic to want to be loved and respected. We all want to be desired or admired in one way or another, but no one is going to do that to a person that does not think that way about themselves. While I was like that, I not only felt the pain inside that a lack of self-respect offered. I also felt the pain of rejection that followed by those who would see me as an invisible character or someone that they had labelled a lost cause. Both experiences were a choice, designed by my being and the only person who could get me out of that was me. I am glad to say I now have the respect of thousands of people due to how I managed to turn my life around, and in doing so, use the experience of that time to assist others in the prevention of Drug Abuse.

A person is not born with respect; they have to earn it, and it took me a while to realise that and then get mine back. I am now sought after for my knowledge of those times and the work I currently do. Yes, you can lose your self-respect and the respect of others, but when you go about quietly changing your situation for the better, those people that used to avoid you start coming back out of the woodwork to show their approval and respect. It is a great feeling, but the greatest feeling of all is that you have regained your self-respect. You put the work in, and you earned it and that my friends are worth anyone's respect.

I also have a deep respect for others, no matter their circumstance. Before, I never understood the importance of that, but as you age, you realise respect for others is as important as respect for yourself. Besides, no one is going to have respect for a person that does not have respect for them. I have since come to the conclusion that everyone on this planet is here for a purpose and each and every one of us are at different stages within our journey. We have all been in similar positions at one time or another, and so, therefore, it is wise not to pass judgement on any person; now that is being respectful.

Exercise: Now, this will require pure honesty on your part. Look in the mirror and ask yourself, what is it you like about yourself and what is it you don't like about yourself? Write it down in your journal. Start with the obvious good stuff first and then proceed to write down all the non-visible stuff, such as how you are as a person.

How you think others see you. Are your relationships with others Caring, Sharing, Kind, Positive, Appreciative, Happy, Informative, Encouraging, Inspiring, Co-operative, Communicative, Supportive, Respectful? Like I said, you have to be really honest. When you write this list down, tick the things that you are happy with about yourself and the ones that you are not so happy with and you feel could use some work, put a question mark against. The exercise is to actively and positively upgrade each area that needs work on. Take time to master each one until you see results from others and within yourself. It may be that you are short-tempered or shout a lot, which is in itself disrespectful to both you and the recipient. Look for ways in which you can better those areas in your life that do not resonate with deep respect. Practice doing things differently. If you are a person that flies off the handle easily, then instead of losing your temper, take a deep breath and count to 20 in your head. It will give you time to look at the situation in a calmer manner and possibly make a better form of response.

RESONANCE

"Resonance happens when your mind and heart come into sync."

[Ravindra Shukla]

Have you ever read a book that when you read it, you are so in tune with what it is saying that you almost think the book is speaking to you at that particular moment? Well, that's you resonating with its meaning. You have that flash where you resonate with what you read, and you just get charged inside. It's like that personal *'me too'* feeling, or *'I have always thought that.'* When you agree with someone's thought or idea, you are said to be "on the same wavelength" or "in resonance with" that person; you resonate with what they are saying. I never knew what it was to resonate with something until I branched out from my limiting environment and took ownership of my own life where, on my travels, I stumbled upon people, books, and even environments that I felt a certain resonance with. That *in tune* moment where I just felt warm inside and yet not many people talk about the importance of this practice. When you resonate with something, you are in a moment of clarity and understanding, and it seems to awaken something inside that encourages you to look deeper into what it is you have resonated with. For me, it is like a sort of synchronistic confirmation that I am on the right path. It is almost like some ethereal hand has guided me towards a certain book, chapter, person, or a place that allows me to experience this resonance and leads me onto other books, which then leads me onto other people and in turn adds to an all-round better experience within my life. I am currently in two 'WhatsApp' groups, and I got there by venturing out of my comfort zone and searching for something different, where I figured there was a strong possibility I would end up meeting like-minded people. My decision paid off, and it has now added a positive boost to my journey. I am well on the way to writing my first few books, including this one, with the *intention* of inspiring others who may be at a crossroads in life to do the same. I now spend much of my time in places where I know that there will be conversations with people that I will resonate with, libraries, seminars, and nature. Nature is also a huge one for me as I believe it to be a great friend to us all if we only allow it. To be able to observe the beauty of nature is a gift that I am so very grateful for. My local park is huge, beautiful, and full of life; my soul just feels calm around the trees, birds, squirrels and other people who also resonate with the dance of nature. It's so beautiful to find things that you resonate with, for that act can only enhance your life and take you on a journey of discovery that will guide you to your destination.

Exercise: Write a list in your journal of friends that you resonate with or that you have incredible uplifting or mind-expanding conversations with. If you are fortunate to have any like this, then make a plan to spend more time with them doing things that will expand things you are both in tune with. If you do not have any friends like this, then ask yourself, where can you find people with similar interests? Go to the library or bookstore and check out books that inspire you into action. If you cannot afford them, then sit and read a chapter a day. It's free to read a book in-house, I did that for years when I was strapped for cash and found that I resonated with many of the authors on the self-help section, which if I am honest probably saved my life. Nature, go out every day, preferably before midday or even on your lunch break to the local park or in the leafier part of your locality and just sit on the bench. A calmness will follow suit and refresh you for the rest of your day; it will recharge your batteries, preparing you for your next task of the day. When we join nature, it is wise to carry a pen and journal as it is these tranquil moments that we get our best flashes of inspiration. To be in tune with nature is to resonate with our higher selves, as the act of doing so will astound you. If you are unable to leave your home, then the internet has a wealth of information that you will most certainly be able to resonate with. It is the world wide web for that very reason, to offer information to those searching for knowledge, answers, and such-like.

RE-INVENT

"When things are bad, it's the best time to reinvent yourself."

[George Lopez]

Fear stops us from wanting to reinvent ourselves, to reinvent yourself is to pursue change, and not many people like change because of the fear of failure, or what others may think. But if you look in the mirror and don't like what you see, then reinvent. You must, if you want to see different results. I cannot count the number of times I have reinvented myself over the years, but on reflection, I can honestly say that I am glad that I did, as it has turned me into an interesting character in the eyes of many and, on a personal level, has shown me how resilient I can actually be. I have chosen to reinvent myself when I am tired of a role that I find no longer serves me or when the chips are down and no longer work in my favour. To reinvent yourself is to show the world that you are not a one-trick pony and that you have many facets to your being. It's also refreshing to come out with a new you. When a person looks in the mirror, and they decide that they are fed up with their hairstyle, they trot off to the salon and reinvent their look. It usually is a serious transformation and is observed by many who will no doubt have verbal input into how the new you is looking. In my lifetime, I have been many things, and these many things required me at times to change my look, all of which I have accumulated numerous experiences from, which I now use to help others. There were also times where I was offered opportunities that would also require me to change or reinvent myself either in look or even in attitude. Eric Thomas once said, ***"If you are not where you want to be, do not quit, instead reinvent yourself and change your habits."*** I did that and found that it works. If you are stuck at a crossroads wondering what to do next, then choose to be something different. Would you like to be an artist, Singer, Poet, Musician, Mother, Father, Teacher, Sports Personality, Writer, Community Leader, etc.? Whatever it is you choose, work towards making that new you happen; re-invent yourself.

EXERCISE: Look into your past and notice how many changes you have made in your life, from birth to the current date. If you are not the same person that you were 20 years ago, then chances are you know about reinventing yourself? Write the list down as you will discover you have inadvertently worn many hats throughout that time. Now that you know, you have done this, make a conscious choice to reinvent yourself into whatever you fancy, followed with the question. What can I do today that will get me nearer my goal of becoming ....? The answer will always come to you if the question is sincere.

CHAPTER 5

VISION

If you see yourself negatively, then that's how others will see you also. You are what you think, and what you think is what you attract. Once you understand this fully, you then come to realise that it is you who creates your world; from this realisation, you then have a choice. We are all where we are in life because of the choices we make. Once we grasp that truth, then it makes sense to feed our mind with a vision of things more conducive to our wellbeing; things that will benefit us, uplift our spirit and encourage us to be the best we can be. It's not rocket science, but it is a science in itself. Once you grasp this knowledge, you will see how simple it is and start to apply it to your life immediately because, let's face it, no one wants to be unhappy in the world and all of us deep down want to be loved. That being the case, it makes sense to focus on feeding the mind with things that will promote self-worth. It took me years to realise this simple truth because I had so many beliefs about myself that were indoctrinated into my brain. My Mother used to say things like, "You make me sick, I hate you; Get out of my sight, You are ugly; You're not as pretty as your sister, no man will want to be with you; No one will want to hear what you have to say," and the list of negativity thrown my way would go on daily. What you learn to believe as a child does affect you in the future. Those sort of words stick in mind and take a long time to come to terms with. Not surprisingly, I suffered severe low self-esteem and, as such, shied away from numerous opportunities that passed my way. I went down the route of taking drugs for quite a few years to possibly dampen the inner pain of always feeling worthless. The vision of myself in those early days led to me detracting from my path toward a slip road to destruction where I lost my way. But that was then, and this is now, and I am pleased to say that, today, I am a different person because I finally made a choice; I chose to live. I started to take life into my own hands and stop being a victim. I started to look at myself as someone that could be of some help to people using the knowledge that I had gained within my lifetime. I started to view myself as a creative mentor that would be able to share experiences that would encourage others to walk a better path. I have gone from poor me to lucky me as every experience has strengthened me and made me who I am today. I am now known amongst many of my friends as one of the most positive people they know. Wayne Dyer once said, ***"When you change the way you look at things, the things you look at change."*** It is one of my favourite sayings, as each time I practice this, it works every single time. So changing your vision into something that you would like to see happening for you is one of the most important things you can do for yourself. It is the greatest gift you can give you, and guess what? It's FREE.

EXERCISE: You will need a pen, pad, and notice board: First of all, write down a list of the things that you would like to see manifest in your life, so if it's something to do with, let's say relationships, you might want to title that one area RELATIONSHIPS and then pin that on the notice board. Truly think about the word, then expand on what you mean regarding what you hope to have within all your future relationships with people. On mine, I put down the following: Honest, caring, responsible, empathic, loving, kind, gentle, collaborative, supportive, respectful, sharing, helpful, reassuring, understanding, inspiring, positive, open, appreciative, concerned, connected. I then looked at what I had written and, in turn, looked at who in my current circle was not a match to what I had written. It certainly made me look at things differently and this simple exercise empowered me to slowly distance myself from people that were no longer a match to my future expectations regarding relationships: I may see these people once in a while, but no longer are they in a position to affect my life in a negative manner as I have since moved on through choosing a new vision for my future. Going back to the notice board, try and find 6 main categories that you would like to see changed for the better, so if it's a car you want, then see yourself in that car. What I did with mine was to cut out the picture of the car that I wanted, then I also cut a picture out of my head and shoulders, adding it to the car. Before I go to bed, I look at all of the images and words I have put on the notice board or Vision Board and talk through each category to my higher self as though they were sitting next to me. I talk about the importance of having these things in my life, and in doing this, I change my line of thinking, which in turn changes my vision for the better. Look in the mirror and ask yourself honestly what it is you love about you? Is there anything at all that you don't, and if so, do what you can to change any negative view you may have about you. May I also suggest listening to 'I AM' affirmations on YouTube as a way of helping you to change your vision from dark to light. **"Vision without action is merely a dream. Action without vision just passes the time. Vision with action can change the world." [Joel A. Barker]**

VIBRATION

"If you want to find the secrets of the universe, think in terms of energy, frequency, and vibration."

[Nikola Tesla]

Ever heard the saying, I'm getting bad vibes from him/her/them/that? That is because everything is vibration, and it is the intention behind the vibration that makes it run at a certain frequency. If I make an intention to harm something, then I will be sending out bad vibes. If I make an intention to remain miserable for no reason, then my vibration is going to be running at a low, and if I make a choice to walk into a room full of people who are arguing and fighting amongst themselves, then I am choosing to rub shoulders with people that are shedding bad vibes and those vibes will affect me in some way or other. The only way to avoid them is to do something that might raise my vibration. My Mother was a person that could not help spreading bad vibes amongst her children, playing one off against the other was one of her favourite pastimes, and of course, the vibrations were felt in fear of being rejected by not only my mother, but the siblings also. I understood from an early age that bad vibes were something that I didn't like and that was to be avoided at all times. Unfortunately, my mother was treated really badly as a child, and so she went on to do the same to me and some of the other siblings. Bad vibes were rife in our house and totally different from the children's home, I was in before being sent back to my mother. I never understood why Social Services would want to put me back into such a negative environment, but they did. The Children's home, however, produced good vibes where everything was done with care and love, a stark contrast from the parental home. The two energies or should I say vibrations were dark and light, chalk and cheese, and gave me a clear understanding of how I would like to see myself in the future. I always wanted to be the complete opposite of my Mother who was unhappy, angry, bitter, scathing, paranoid, and cruel. I am positive, happy, creative, inquisitive, and have a thirst for knowledge. I am always being asked out to attend this or that party or event because of the positive vibes I omit. Sadly, for my Mother, I cannot remember a time I really ever saw her out with any friends. I put that down to her vibration, her energy.

Exercise: Write down 20 things that make you feel bad, then write another 20 that make you feel joyous. Do all you can to avoid all the things that make you feel bad as they are having a negative effect on your vibrations. Expand on all the ones that make you feel joyous and do all you can to keep your vibrations raised. Not only is it better for your health, but it also raises your popularity as you are seen as a blessing to be around.

VISION BOARD

I never understood until recently the importance of creating and using a vision board for my advantage. But today, I can honestly say that if I had the power, I would bring this simple but very effective tool into every classroom. I would start the week off with getting people to dream and spend the whole morning getting them to experience the feeling of their dreams/visions. By doing that, I would be helping them to open up a channel in their minds that would possibly align them with circumstances that would lead them towards the path of the vision they have created. In schools, we are taught academic, finite stuff, much of which will possibly have no use in our adult life. But we are never taught how to dream, how to feel successful, how to become successful using the tools of our magnificent imaginations all of which are infinite. We are never taught to visualise a better future. This year, I created a vision board as I have had positive results in the past where I have visualised events, friendships, and such-like that have all since transpired. Those visualisations were in mind only, but if you create a Vision Board, then that would make those manifestations come quicker as not only will you be able to view something tangible, but you will also put what you see back into your imagination and build on it from there. Seeing is believing. I gave myself a task, and I looked online for the house that I see my future self living in. I dreamt big on this one as I know my mind is infinite, so I am not scared to think that way. I found the house I would like along with the rooms, gardens, home gym, library room, even down to the two hairless cats Hector and Suzy, Red e-type jaguar car, etc. I put as much detail into that as I could. I put it all together and then printed off a couple of copies; one which I put in my daily journal so as I can see it first thing and throughout the day, and the other one I put up where I can see it just before I go to sleep at night. Each time I look at the dream home, I imagine myself in the garden and who I will be entertaining there, feeding the birds and planting new flowers, or working out in the home gym, or taking a whole day out to just sit in my private library reading my latest favourite book. This is, of course, make-believe stuff, but it is also very powerful as what it does is stop you thinking about anything negative and opens pathways that attract ways of you getting what it is that you feel. It's like being a child again, you go into this make-believe world and start letting your imagination run wild. In your mind, you can have, be, or do anything you want and as long as it hurts no one, then there is no reason why you cannot obtain this in real life. It is all in the seeing and feeling. The biggest plus of all when creating a vision board for me is that when I am in that mode of creation, I apply my whole self to it and become a new me. The me that I would like to be with the things that I would like to have and the places that I would like to visit along with the special friends and family members that I want around me. Vision Boards are not only a tool to help you to get what it is you wish for, but it also manages to provide you with positive food for thought and offers you a spoonful of hope for the future. Recently, I had something on my mind that I wanted to get rid of as it was negative and I felt uneasy about the whole thing, so I deliberately focused my attention on my dream house and spent much time adding more detail to it, which conjured up happy feelings. When you are in the mode of good feeling, bad feeling has no way of getting in, and so now I use vision boards for the purpose of also keeping negative thoughts at bay. Vision Boards allow you to actively see what you can possibly achieve; they are what dreams are made of. If you saw it in your mind's eye, then it is not impossible to get or achieve. When you create your Vision Board, you will also find it quite therapeutic not to mention fun.

'Whatever the mind can conceive, you can achieve.' And if your mind conceives the things that you most want, then you are on the way to manifesting your dreams by putting out a clear intention on what it is that you would like to see happening in your life. There are some incredible stories of people who swear by this action that has not only manifested their visions, but has also gone to become leaders in their field for doing so. A Vision Board keeps your eyes on the prize, it promotes a renewed way of thinking, and it's fun to do and depending on how much you focus on the belief that what you have created is actually yours, it gives you something to strive for. It also stops you from thinking of anything negative. It's all about making your visions or dreams a reality, living the dream. Every time you look at your vision and deeply believe that it is yours, you bring that into your conscious mind, who in turn brings it to the subconscious, which is where all the magic happens. The secret is in the feeling, and without that feeling, nothing that you visualise will transpire. It is important, therefore, to realise that there are a few things in play here. First comes the thought, which are the images, then once you are satisfied with these, then put yourself in the picture until you feel the vibrations of being there. The best time to do this is the last thing at night as this is where the subconscious works at its best. There is a book out there by 'Neville Goddard' called 'The Feeling Is The Secret,' and it explains in great detail this little known fact that if we were to apply it to all things in our lives, we would not want for anything else again in our own lives.

Anyone that has a dream can create a vision board.

Exercise: Create eight or nine categories that you would like to add to your vision board. On mine, I have the following: Career, Spiritual, Wealth, Health, Family, LOVE, Relationships, Home, Travel. Each category I chose, I found a picture to match and then I added words that I felt were beneficial to my future wellbeing. An example of that would be **'RELATIONSHIPS'** and what I would require within it. I came up with the following: Respect, caring, communicative, understanding, positive, open, helpful, collaborative, well-meaning, honest, appreciative, encouraging, responsible, inspiring, empathy, supportive, loving, community. I look at this regularly and do you know what, because I do that on a regular basis, I no longer tolerate anything less in my life and have since sorted out the wheat from the chaff. It works. So get creating and having fun with this, you will be amazed at the results and make sure that once you have created it, put it up on your wall or a place where you will be able to view it often. Imagine what it would be like to have those sort of relationships, or the career, home, or travel you want. Do not stop looking at the Vision Board until you create a feeling of what it would be like to have those things and then sleep on it. View it again first thing in the morning, adding it to your daily routine always being thankful for having that which you have created.

VALUE

"Understand your worth, value your life, appreciate your blessings."

[Anonymous]

Growing up, I suffered from severe low self-esteem and often felt worthless and without value due to that negative upbringing. I was never encouraged to feel worthy of anything, and this had a damaging effect on opportunities passed my way and on the way I saw myself. I never ever thought of myself as having value to anyone because I was told at an early age that I was useless, stupid, and ugly. When you grow up being told this on an almost daily basis, a part of you starts to believe it. When something like this is instilled in the mind of a child, how it plays out in later years is quite sad unless, of course, you are able to recognise that which was being told to you was, in fact, a lie. Thank God I took to reading Self-Help books and watching positive motivational films, which were key in helping me to realise that I do have worth and value. When I look back at the opportunities that came my way that I turned down because I did not value myself enough to take them, it makes me shake my head in disbelief. I laugh now because I also realise that I can use this negative experience positively to assist others. And in this way, I also see that it was indeed a blessing, which I happen to appreciate now.

Many years ago when I was asked about how much I charge for a show, I remember not being able to answer the promoter straight away. The reason for that is because I was unsure of what value to put on myself for what it is that I do. I thought about it for a second and wisely told them I would get back to them the following day. It did, however, make me think why I had not been able to answer that question straight away. For years, I had worked with other people who had dealt with all that for me, but now as a sole trader, it was down to me to work out what value I was able to give a promoter and the audience, or indeed anyone asking for my time, presence, and expertise. That small but very important question was the catalyst to me analysing what I thought I was really worth and what value I would be for others. It took me a while to get it right, and a few errors were made in the process. But after a short while, I became confident in my ability to not waver on my set fee unless, of course, I chose to do so. Initially, I was concerned about being too expensive, then I was equally worried about selling myself too cheap. I then researched others in my field and compared their takings with mine versus what value I had to offer so as I could come up with a worthwhile fee for all involved. More often than not, in the beginning, I would sell myself short, but by doing that, I soon came to realise that I was also devaluing myself. Also, fear of not getting the work because my fees may be too expensive would play tricks on my mind, and that would cause me to drop my prices to possibly suit their agenda; I used to do that, but I don't do that anymore. Fear no longer has a place in any negotiations relating to how I value myself. It took me a long time to realise that if these people were asking for me specifically, then there had to be a reason for it. I had something that possibly others may not have, and so I looked into that further. I recognised that I am worth a lot more than I actually thought just by looking at the situation on a deeper level. I now have the prices for shows and creative workshops valued at the right price for what it is that I can offer. I add into the equation my expertise, time spent in preparation, travel, how many nights I will be away from home and where I am placed on the bill of a show. I also take into consideration their budget before making a definite date.

So the above was about how much you value yourself, but what about time? Time is a highly valuable commodity, but gets wasted on those who don't realise its importance within the great scheme of things. Take procrastination, for instance; when we procrastinate, we lose time, and when time goes, we will never get it back. When I look back on the amount of time I have wasted in the act of procrastination, it saddens me to think how much I could have done if I had valued time in the way I do today. No matter if I am making up for lost time while sharing with others.

EXERCISE: I want you to look at your experiences of life thus far and create a project for anyone you think might benefit from those experiences. Once you have done that, then you need to put a value on it. So say you have created a programme with a view to taking it into places where people have survived trauma and are stuck, then your project will hopefully offer ways of how to inspire those survivors to move on in a positive manner. Your project takes time, maybe it's an afternoon work, put a value on that as it is your time. Create this like it is something that you are going for in the future, and you will be amazed what comes out of this for it will bring some new ideas to the forefront of your mind. What this exercise will do is to open you up to the idea that you do actually have real value to someone or many people and it will also give you a sense of true worth. PLEASE create this and finish the creative project. Make sure you put NO limits on this project, as for now, it is just an exercise.

CHAPTER 6

INTUITION

"Have the courage to follow your heart and intuition. They somehow already know what you truly want to become. Everything else is secondary."

[Steve Jobs]

Has there ever been a time in your life where you have done something with an uneasy feeling? Your heart and head said don't do it, and then you did the opposite only to wish that you had listened to your head? Well, that was your intuition trying to offer you another solution before you decided to go against its guidance. *"To be intuitive means being able to listen, see, hear, or know in ways that complement one's ordinary state of awareness. It involves being receptive or sensitive to that which extends beyond our everyday senses."*

Intuition has to be my dearest and best friend of all time, inner teacher and personal guide. Over these recent years, I have realised that my intuition is actually a secret PA [personal assistant] and it has been assisting me all my life. If I listen to it quite deeply, it never steers me wrong. It has helped me find things that I have misplaced around the home, stopped me from making dangerous choices, made me think about things before taking on certain ventures, guided me to where I needed to go at a particular moment. I have also noticed that when I don't listen to my intuition and go my own way, I usually trip up on my life's journey, which has happened several times throughout my existence on this planet. I have a routine thing I do in the morning where I talk to myself about my plans for the day or even creative ideas for the future, and it never fails to respond. It's like having a magical invisible friend; some people say Intuition is your higher self, your spiritual guide all of which I too believe and I just LOVE the fact that I can call on it to point me in the right direction. Intuition also calls on me and lately, I hear it louder and more consistently. Intuition has also played an amazing part in my poetry and song-writing. It has come up with some fascinating concepts, melodies, and projects. The more I think about its importance in my life, the more I am in awe of its existence. We all have it, but not many talk about it. As I write this, I feel I would like to pay more homage to it in the future given that it could well have saved my life on many occasions, and for this and all the above, I am truly grateful to have Intuition as my best friend and trusted guide. Listen to the voice in your head, when I meditate first thing in the morning when all is quiet, I feel as if I am in tune much stronger than when there is untold noise, headphones on, and people chattering around me all day long. The last thing at night is also a time where I have been known to get some of my greatest ideas for my poetry.

The following WIKIPEDIA quote says it all. "*Intuition is the ability to acquire knowledge without proof, evidence, or conscious reasoning, or without understanding how the knowledge was acquired.*"

EXERCISE: The perfect way to increase your intuition is to meditate; this simple act of stillness increases your awareness. There are so many things online that can show you how to increase your intuition, and this exercise is for you to search for something that will give you a better understanding to tune in. Just Google 'how to become aware of my intuition' and page after page will come up. And if you want to know which one is the best for you, then your intuition will give you the answer as you progress on this journey of discovery. LISTEN, and it shall all be revealed.

INVEST

"The best investment you can make is in yourself."

[Warren Buffett]

I realised the importance of investing in myself a few years ago and have never looked back. By doing so, I have seen many positive results in how I look, feel, act, and create. The change in me since I have invested in me has also been a topic of positive conversation with my peers and new people I have met. Coupled with some discipline, I went on to make some severe changes within my life. As I was serious about investing in myself, I realised I had to sacrifice a few things that I had become too comfortable with. I made the decision to stop hanging out with people that were taking up too much of my time and energy. I gave up drinking, cigarettes, slimmed down on the socialising, politely deleted people out of my life that were either a bad influence or a negative drain on my energy and replaced what I had sacrificed with something better. Drink and cigarettes were replaced with hitting the gym at 6.00 am 5-6 days a week. Socialising was replaced with staying at home and writing poetry and creating new projects. TV was replaced with reading and writing books and going within myself in meditation. I even became a Vegan and have never looked or felt better in myself. It was a decision to invest in me and one I will never look back on. It took me a while to give up the things that were no longer positively serving me, and I didn't do it all in one go. Actually, I gave up TV first, then a year later meat, 2 years after that dairy, then I started to get bored with socialising for the sake of it, so I slimmed it down dramatically and opted for going to a poetry event once a month. I love hanging with like-minded people that have something to say, and once every few months, I may attend a 1 - 4-day seminar on how to achieve greater things, or promote a more positive mindset or gain new skills beneficial to my life's purpose.

When you invest in yourself, you make a decision to become a better version of yourself, and as you work at it, you start feeling what you are becoming, and when you feel better about yourself, then it shows and others around you notice a difference. You begin to value your time, mind, body, soul, and health. A drug addict invests in the dealer, the addict makes a choice to feed the addiction, but in doing so, he is not positively investing in him/herself and the only one getting the benefit of that investment is the dealer; financially. That also applies to any addict be it drugs, sex, alcohol, workaholic, or gambling, all those actions eventually deplete the energy of the spirit. But when you invest in just you, and the betterment of you, then you decide to upgrade and reprogramme your very being. You are your greatest investment, and if you are thinking of becoming an entrepreneur, then investing in yourself before you do so is a must. No one will want to invest in a person that does not know how to invest in themselves. If some of the sacrifices I took resonate with you, then please follow suit, as you will notice a positive difference if you do.

EXERCISE: May I suggest you start the exercise by looking at your friends' list and do some housecleaning in that area. Friends will come and go throughout our lifetime, and we just have to accept that. So, you have to be brutally honest here. Are all your friends amazing, and if there are some that rile you, then maybe it's time to ease them out. You are investing in yourself when you surround yourself with like-minded people that can elevate your spirit, not bring you down. Areas of your life that you must look at for investing in your future are as follows:

- ✓ Food - Is what you eat healthy?
- ✓ Health - Fitness - How fit and healthy are you?
- ✓ Happiness - Are you happy right now?
- ✓ Love life - What can you do to improve that or acquire one?
- ✓ Environment - Are you happy with where you are right now?
- ✓ Friendships - Are they wholesome, caring, loving, respectful, engaging, and beneficial?
- ✓ Current Job - Does it excite you to go there every day? If not, where would you like to be in 5 years from now?

Be honest with yourself about the above list and go through every point one by one. **On Food**, make a list of how much sugar is involved in that food. Look at the labels of the food you do buy and see if they have E numbers, (which by the way I avoid at all costs as it is not clear what is in these, and I don't eat what I don't understand). Maybe you could find healthy alternatives if your diet is laced with biscuits, cakes, puddings, crisps and other such fattening foods, replace with fruits and watch the difference. **On Health**, ask yourself how fit you are and what you are doing to maintain that level of fitness. Are you already someone that gets fit in the gym or are you someone that always looks in the mirror and says, "I'm going to join the local gym soon," but has never stepped foot inside one in all the years of promising to do so? NOW is the time, as wishing is just a pipe dream. **On Happiness,** you have to be honest here; are you happy? And if you are not, then what is causing this unhappiness? Could it be the current job? Relationship? The list is endless here, and only you know the answer to how you can regain that happiness. Decide to alleviate the pressures that are bringing you down and holding you back and stopping you from being the person that you have always wanted to be. **On Love,** are you being honest with yourself about your relationship with the main person in your life, which is YOU? How much do you love yourself? Do you look in the mirror and say, ugh, I'm too fat, too thin, not pretty enough, my hair's a mess, I need toning up, and the list goes on. Look at each area of that and start to get positive with yourself. First of all, if there is something that you don't like about you, then you can always change it. If you are unable to love yourself, then you cannot expect someone to love you in the way you would like to be loved. Work on loving yourself and may I also suggest finding some positive affirmations and listening to them first thing in the morning every single day for the next month or until they sink into your psyche. Start looking into loving you from today. **On your Environment:** If you don't like where you are right now, then ask yourself one question. "What steps can I take to get me out of where I am right now?" I guarantee that an answer leading you towards getting out of that situation will come. If you set the intention in your head that you have had enough and would like to leave the situation, then you will be amazed at the outcome as the universe will conspire to help you to leave wherever it is you are unhappy with. Of course, you will need to start thinking of ways yourself that might see you taking flight from the environment you no longer wish to be in. But if the suggestion of thought about leaving does not enter the mind, then you will remain where you are, as the subconscious will assume that you are happy where you are. See yourself somewhere else and chances are, with this daily practice, things will start to change for you. The art of making the changes, however, also comes with a belief that you CAN change your environment and a feeling that you can be in the place of your dreams. [Read or listen to 'Feeling Is The Secret' by Neville Goddard]

INSPIRE

"Be the inspiration you are looking for."

[Jennie Matthias]

Sometimes when I am a little stuck, I look for things that have inspired me back into action. My intuition plays a great part in guiding me in finding the right thing that I need to assist me in this area. It works every time, especially when you are in tune with this. With technology the way it is, with a click of the button, you can become inspired into action. Once inspired, you are hooked into a frequency of wellbeing with a raised vibration, and the key is to remain in that zone, which may see you search for more things to inspire you. I remember when I was new to all this, I would read books that would inspire me as the internet was not around the way it is now. When I found a book that totally resonated with me, I would be inspired enough to get a thirst on for more of the same or similar, unbeknown to me I was growing my brain and opening my mind up to new possibilities. Since those days, I have built up a fabulous library of books that have not just inspired me, but others also as I LOVE sharing wisdom with others. Each morning without fail, I click on the morning I AM Affirmations, and they become the backdrop to my getting prepared for the gym. While you are listening to positive affirmations, there is no way that you can feel down. The only way you can feel is happy and inspired to go through your day with a positive attitude, and the key to keeping this level of vibrancy up is to go throughout your day repeating the affirmations to yourself. In the past, I have been known to let things that go on throughout the day get to me, either a harsh word from someone, a headline on the Yahoo news, overhearing negative gossip, etc. But nowadays, I avoid all that, as I have trained myself to think quietly about things that inspire me or lift my spirit. I have since become such a dab hand at searching for things that inspire me that I have shared these moments of inspiration with others that I felt needed it. I have gone from being the person that searches for inspiration to being the person who now inspires others into action, offering them a glimpse into the world of vibrant spirit, which is actually what we all are. But many of us allow life to bring us down or get us lost in a fog, or stuck on the same old treadmill. To get off of that, one needs to become inspired again. When you become an inspired person, people notice the change in you, and when you become a person that inspires others with what you now know, then you become a person that people simply love to have in their company because, at the end of the day, everyone LOVES to be inspired by something. Inspiration, when act upon, is the catalyst to a better life, and if you bring inspirational moments into your daily rituals [especially if it's first thing in the morning and last thing at night], chances are you will find many ways to keep you from ever getting stuck in the fog of life again. Some people leave the country looking to be inspired, and then there are those that look towards others that they have seen develop positively. Some search for Gurus to inspire them spiritually and mentally; others like me seek out uplifting friendships, write poetry, read and write books to inspire myself and others.

Exercise: a) Go to YouTube and search for I AM affirmations for morning and then night. Choose the ones that inspire you and play it in the morning and then the night, for the morning affirmations just follow what they are saying and repeat after them. Do this for a whole month until the words sink into your psyche. b) Watch what you're doing in conversations with others, are you listening to or sharing negative gossip? If you then know that there is NOTHING inspirational about that activity and if inspiration is what you truly desire, then take a look at the list of friends that you do have. Write them down in your journal, and put a tick beside which ones inspire you the most. If you are unable to find any, then it's time to re-think your friends' list. Hanging out with the right people can be fruitful in the area of inspiration, especially when a conversation about things that you like is talked about with enthusiasm and passion. You are inspired by these people to hang with them a tad more as their very being lifts you up and your conversations with them not only inspire you, but you also inspire them. c) Inspire yourself by learning a new craft, whether it's to play the guitar, learn how to swim, write a poetic sketch from start to finish, you will be so amazed that you have finished it that you will most certainly be inspired into writing another one.

INVOLVE

You have to be in it to win it; that way, you not only get to meet new people, but you may pick up new skills, ideas, and even lasting friendships. It is imperative you get out there and get involved if you wish to grow. When I was an addict, I spent my time with other addicts, but when I decided to disassociate myself from them, I found it scary to step into environments I had never graced before. While I was nursing myself back to health, it was a lonely time, which was a choice I made as I felt that solitude was the only way I could clean my act up fast. After a while, though I chose to step out into the world again with a fresh head and body, and had a yearning for meeting new people. I decided to volunteer some of my time to a local charity who was crying out for help. It was a women's charity, and many of the women there had suffered extreme violence in their own countries and were here to seek asylum. I just had to get involved with this; it was completely out of my comfort zone to volunteer in a place where I was unsure if I had anything to offer, but what experience I did have I was willing to share as I just felt in my heart that this was a truly worthy cause. It so happened that there were many skills that I had picked up along my journey of life that enabled me to assist these incredible women. I am an avid reader and writer, fast typist, songwriter, motivator of people, brave when speaking out for others, which was a great asset at this place as we would often go on marches to make others aware of the injustices of certain situations pertaining to women's rights. I was able to take notes, cut up newspaper articles, and I even got the ladies to assist me with writing a song for their campaign by using their wording to get the messages across. By getting involved, I was able to help this very hardworking charity where I have made lifelong friends and who I still see to this very day. Priceless and a complete eye-opener for me. On a personal level, I also felt a bit sad about having spent time away from the world due to my unhealthy choices. I had a wake-up moment where I just felt so selfish. I had spent years destroying myself on class A's, not caring whether I lived or died, just going through the motions of life and there were these ladies that had lost their families, homes. Many had been physically, mentally, and sexually assaulted in the most heart-rendering circumstances, and I just woke up and promised myself that I would NEVER EVER be that selfish being again. There are people out there that need help. By getting involved, I was able to view life differently. It was no longer about me; it was now about clearing the slate, starting again and seeing what I could do to assist those in greatest need, those that would appreciate any of the skills I had to offer. By getting involved, I changed my world for the better. I have since gone on to involve others in all sorts of amazing ventures. I also became a mentor for a few young people that were struggling to cope with their current circumstances, and being a survivor of harsh early life experiences, I felt best placed to assist in that area. I would say that my decision to get involved with helping that local clarity was the catalyst in helping me to get where I find myself today. That one simple act changed my world and helped me to change the world of others also. It helped me to recognise and realise that I do have some worth and that there are people out there that would appreciate that worth. When you involve yourself with different people, you allow yourself to become stimulated with new ideas, new ways of thinking and working. I am forever grateful for making that choice and for being shown the truth about what I was and what I could become to others; I have never looked back, and I am still helping the ladies out from time to time using my song-writing skills for them to get their messages across in a more pleasing way.

Exercise: This exercise will require you to get out of your comfort zone and do something totally different. I am convinced that going down a similar route to the one I went down will offer you similar results or more.

Look for a charity that resonates with you, whether it be animals, people with disabilities, hospitals, old people's homes, feeding the homeless, working on the environment, etc. It's all down to what speaks to your heart. Make a commitment to assist once a week or fortnight. When you call up, let them know that you are committing to this for their charity and make an appointment to see them. Charities are crying out for volunteers and would relish any help. You will be amazed by what this does for your self-worth. When you involve yourself in this way, you are appreciated for taking the time to care enough to help. People usually go where they are appreciated, you never know, this could be the catalyst for finding out your 'Life's Purpose.'

INTENTION

"Intention is the seed that creates the future."

[Anonymous]

When you set an intention and are clear about what it is you actually want, all you have to do is focus on it 100%. Do not let distractions, doubt, or anything else steer you away from that which you have intended. The intention you set has to, of course, be something that you enjoy and truly want to do. Intention is the starting point of all your dreams. Everything that happens with us starts with our intention, no matter how big or small. When we walk the dog on the beach, go to the park, shops, on holiday, drive in the car, go to a club, that all starts with an intention. My intention right here and now is to finish off this book and start on the next one. It is something that I intend to do, am currently doing, and am focusing on the outcome. What also comes with that is the feeling of what achieving that aim would reveal. I have an image in my mind of that intention, and then during the journey of that intention, it expands, grows legs, and becomes a grand masterpiece, and this is even before I started that which I intend. I first intend, and then the imagery of that intention builds and builds, and it becomes a reality before I even start and it's this that sets me on that journey to truly build on my intention. When I take my friend's dog on the beach, it is my intention to take it first thing in the morning and last thing at night. It is something I do not waver from. I have it in my mind's eye that this is the most important thing that I do when I go visit this friend because I LOVE the dog and promised him that when I was in town that I would be the one to give him extra special long quality walks and runs on the beach. I intended that this should happen and it has happened in exactly the way I intended. Because I have a strong affection for this dog, it is easy for me to keep my focus on my initial intention. I realise how important for him this is, and so it is important for me also. When I am at home, my biggest intention is to build on ideas pertaining to my life's purpose. When I initially intended to sit down and add life to this intention, it was just a spark of an idea in my head. It has since grown and grown, and at times I feel as though I cannot keep up with all the ideas relating to building on this. What started out as an idea and then my intention to see that idea through has brought me to a new world of thought and discovery. It has guided me to people who can assist me in enhancing this intention, and it has allowed me to understand the importance of staying focused on my intention. The Empire State Building didn't just appear on the New York landscape, someone intended it to happen. The journey after that became a gargantuan project, and what you see today is a record of that journey. One idea is just one idea, but unless you INTEND to put feeling, emotion, and imagery to it, then it will always remain, just an idea. What is it that you are passionate about, so passionate that you can see what it is, feel, smell, and observe yourself doing it?

EXERCISE: Get a brand new journal for this one and title it INTENTION, as when an idea you want to bring into fruition, an idea that you intend to make happen comes into the forefront of your mind. You will catch yourself building on these ideas that will inspire you further to make that intention come alive. The key is to remain totally focused. Even if it is just 1 - 4 hours a day, you must make sure you are consistent with it. Just do it and watch what happens.

INFORMATION

"The more information you have on where it is you are headed in your life, the greater the chance of reaching your destination."

[Jennie Matthias]

We are living in a world where information has never been so accessible; they don't call it the World Wide Web for nothing, we are no longer limited by lack of knowledge in the way we have been in the past. Anything that we want to know can be found at the click of a button. Computers are everywhere, much in the same way TVs are, and have become an essential part of how we communicate with each other. If you don't have one, then there are internet cafes who charge a small fee for using their computers or better still you can get free usage from the library. The benefit of using a computer from the library is that you are in a peaceful environment, surrounded by books, with the untapped knowledge waiting to be discovered. At the click of a button, you can have all your questions answered.

I have been healed by information on the net, and my mind has expanded into all sorts of areas from spiritually to world news and views. It has most certainly replaced the TV (from which I am proud to say I have not watched in 1 year) as I find it so much more interesting and the best thing about it all is that you get to choose the information you soak in. My quest for knowledge has opened new pathways, helping me to create some fabulous artistry such as poetry, prose, songs, etc. It has also given me insight into a different world than the one I was led to believe as once being true. My thirst for knowledge is immense, and before the internet became popular, I could see a time where it would be used in the way it is now and so I enrolled on a course at a technical college. That decision paid off as the skills enabled me to access so much more information than I could ever have imagined possible. Ignorance can NO longer be an excuse these days. Nearly everyone on this planet can access information now, so what are you waiting for? Get up and at it and use whatever information you are seeking to assist you in your life's purpose.

EXERCISE: Search the internet for information that will upgrade your understanding of why it is you exist within this universe. Though this is just an exercise, it will give you some remarkable results and serious food for thought. The WWW has a knack of leading you down many paths, which in turn add to the initial information sought after.

VOICE

"Leadership is finding your voice, inspiring others to find their voice, empowering people and executing actions that make the world better."

[Anyaele Sam Chison]

Once you find your voice, you can then go on and be a voice for others. My mother was never encouraging; she used to tell me how ridiculous I sounded and that no one would ever listen to what I had to say. It's not surprising then that I grew up with severe low self-esteem. I had no voice; I was shy and timid and used to let people walk all over me as I was too afraid to speak up for myself. It was only when I ventured into the world of performance (which by the way initially was not an easy task) that I was able to find my voice, and although that took time, it helped me to then become a voice for others. It helped that the platform offered to me to share my voice with others was that of entertainment, and this made it easier to deal with. In those days, I was new to the world of singing in front of hundreds if not thousands of people, and then there were TV cameras and shows, which would go out to millions of people. I was a regular on Top Of The Pops, which was the biggest music programme in the UK, so I went from this girl who wouldn't say boo to a goose, to this larger than life figure who people actually wanted to listen to. I could never understand why, but I enjoyed the ride anyway. In between the songs on live performances, I eventually came into my own as being the lead singer for a famous pop group. I had to keep an audience motivated and interested while introducing the next song. It ended up being such fun, and in due course, I found my voice; the one I was told no one would want to hear.

I am happy to say that I now have a long list of numerous achievements on how I have used my voice to benefit those in greatest need, and as such, I am a strong advocate for those who, like me, struggled to be heard. Finding your voice will require you to get out of your comfort zone. But this is the way of life, how will we ever learn to fly if we never take that initial step to jump off the cliff? There have been numerous occasions where I have positioned myself in many scenarios, where I have spoken up for those whose voices are never heard. As a Vegan, I speak up for the animals and their rights, I involve myself in marches against animal cruelty, I have worked with adults and disability and have been the voice for them when it comes to getting their rights aired in the public domain. I have been very creative with getting the message out there to the people on Anti-War marches, using their literature to turn into a song where literally thousands of people can join in. Once you find your voice, there is no turning back; you will want to use it not only to help yourself, but to help others also. At the beginning of this book, you would have seen my poem 'SURVIVE.' I wrote that from my heart and have been truly blessed to have found venues where audiences have listened to those words, and every time I have done so, you can hear a pin drop in the room. Words and delivery inspire others, and I feel my life's journey has set me up to become a master speaker to help the masses raise vibration. I found my voice, and you too can find your voice.

Exercise: This will require you to be brave, but you will be inspired into finding your voice when you see and hear others doing the same.

Go online and look up local open mic nights where they do 'Spoken Word.' These are usually free, and if not, then just a few quid. Bring your pen and pad as you will most definitely be inspired into some form of action. Either go there on your own or with a friend and view each performer. There are usually performers that either do poetry or prose and they all have something to say. Many of them talk about their experiences from the past, and others talk about their observations. Most of them are new at this and are just trying out new material to see if an audience would be interested in listening to what they have to say. It is one of the best ways I know for a person to get involved in expressing themselves. You see, everyone has something to say and usually wants to do just that, but not many realise that there are platforms out there that will enable them to be heard. Most of the people are just starting out and have never even used a mic before; you will find this encouraging. It might be scary at first, but as a mentor to young upcoming artists, I am a strong advocate of 'Practice Makes Perfect.' Once you write just one small poem or prose, then practice it to perfection so as you can read it without the paper as only then will you be ready to share what you have on the mic. I guarantee you that it will inspire you to make more of your voice and use it to its best advantage.

VOLUNTEER

"The heart of a volunteer is never measured in size, but by the depth of the commitment to make a difference in the lives of others"

[Anonymous]

If, like me, you grew up believing you were worthless, then I can assure you that this was a lie. You are needed somewhere in this world, and there are charitable services that would relish your knowledge or experience or skills. It does not matter how big or small; they will be more than happy to have you volunteer your time. All you need is enthusiasm. When you volunteer your time for others, you get involved with people whom you would never have met before making the decision to volunteer. When I chose to volunteer, I thought about what sort of place I would like to go to locally to assist a charity with their daily or monthly plans. I chose to go to the local Women's Centre, where the women were assisting other women that were seeking asylum having gone through the most harrowing of times and often times were used as sex objects or even had witnessed the murder of family and friends at the hands of terror groups. My time there was incredible, and I was just so anxious to assist for what started out as once a week that I said I would do anything that was needed. I also went on to volunteer my time for a homeless charity where we fed over 1,000 healthy hot vegetarian meals to those in greatest need. I stayed there for over 5 years and the skills I gained, not to mention the friends, was beyond measure.

EXERCISE: Volunteer your time to help someone that needs it, whether it be a family member that cannot do much for themselves any more or a charity or a neighbour. This act of kindness will help you to appreciate what you do have in your life.

VICTIM

"We have all been through a lot of shit in our lives; the difference is that some of us choose not to play the victim."

[Anonymous]

Being a victim is a choice one makes, you can either choose a life where it controls you or you can fight back and control your life in the way you wish to and be the go-getter you were born to be. My upbringing taught me a great lesson on this subject, for I have been a victim, and now I am not, it really is that simple. For quite some time, I unconsciously chose to be a victim, but now I am grateful to the powers that be that I no longer have that label. I observed that by being a victim, I was a complete drain on others. It took me a while to realise that, and it did not sit well with me. By being a victim, I was the cause of stress for others, and it was and never will be my reason for being. It took me a while to realise this and a heck of a lot of self-help books to come to terms with what I was doing and I am so glad I did, as by stepping out of victimhood and stepping into taking full control gave me a better understanding of what I had done in the past. I could see traits in me that I had adopted from my mother and knowing how bad she made people feel when they were in her presence. I just wanted NO part of it. My mother was a victim of life and spent her whole life with very few friends. I only knew her to have two friends, and in her later years, she didn't have any; so sad and so unnecessary. My mother was a prime example of someone that had allowed life to control them. She was never happy as a result, and when you are unhappy, you are not in alignment with the planet or yourself, there is no inner harmony. I felt sorry for her, to spend your whole life not knowing harmony is a self-made hell, but it was a choice she made. I know so many people that are still living in the past and at any opportunity are sharing that with anyone that will listen. The only thing that does is make people want to avoid you. When I made the decision to deal with the past and drop it out of the future equation, I gained even more friends, and now I am the total opposite. I have a knack of always finding the silver lining in things and am widely known for my positive persona, a label I prefer far more than that of 'she's a victim.'

When you play the victim card, you run on low vibration, and those on a higher vibration will not want to be around you for too long as, like I said before, they do not want their energy drained, who in their right mind would? I have a friend whose name I shall not mention, who blames what has happened in the past for why she is unable to move forward. She blames everyone but herself for being stuck, and no matter what I say, she does not seem to be able to move away from her line of thinking and progress further. She is also fearful of almost everything, and the backlash of all of this has made her neurotic to the point where people just don't visit her as much anymore. She is resentful of others and has little time to remain in contact with people, as she is too engrossed in her pity party victimhood. As I view her situation, I liken it to my mother's, and it is just so sad as, deep down, this lady has a heart of gold. If you have come from a background where suffering was prevalent, you too might have adopted that victim mentality. It's only natural, and that's okay as long as you recognise that somewhere along your time in life you will have to drop that if you want to progress. Being a victim stunts your growth. Are you the sort of person that feels the need to tell all and sundry about your past experiences? Have people ever made concessions for you as a result of you sharing those experiences? Have you noticed people feeling sorry for you once you have shared your story? If so, then you need to stop that as you are drawing others into your past dramas, and to be frank, it's just needy and simply depressing. You are also feeding yourself with their emotions toward your sad past situation. A victim is NOT a fun person to be around, 100% NOT a person that you invite to parties or too many up-tempo social gatherings. Being a victim of life allows others to label you as a person with issues. You've heard that saying, 'watch out for them, they have issues.' Victims play the poor me card; they say things like, you don't understand, what happened to me never happened to you, how would you know what it's like to have gone through such and such and each of those lines would pave the way for them spilling out their sad story. Unless you are going to use those past experiences of suffering and abuse and put them into good use like teaching others how to survive similar hardships, then it's pointless you are sharing them each time you feel the need to. All you're doing is creating misery for yourself by reliving the moment and putting a downer on someone else's mood. Being a victim keeps you stuck on a low vibration. It is a constant cry for help, and some victims of life use their past experience to seek attention, not realising that they are pushing people away that don't always want to hear those past experiences. If you want to get away from being a victim of life, then please view some of the exercises below. They have worked for me, and if you are honest with yourself, you will see that each thing that happened to you has led you to a certain point. If you are still alive to tell the tale, then the positive outcome of this will show itself, for where there is darkness, there must always be light.

EXERCISE: Your exercise is to write down every bad experience that you ever had [see some of my examples below], and then next to it explain what you have learnt from them because you will have learnt something. You could create a table as I have done below for a lot will pour out of your heart. Before you know it, you will have something that is not only beneficial to you, but others also. I guess that once you start looking deeper on the thing that has been holding you back from progressing, you will eventually embrace those moments as you consciously observe those times from a different perspective. You will then be able to view yourself as a person who has important information that they can use to share with others. In other words, the tools you have gained from the experience of your life will make you an authority. I would rather hear how a survivor used their experience as an opportunity to help others in a similar position than listen to a rerun of the same old story with no movement. Please also re-read the SURVIVE poem in this book for it will give you a greater understanding of how to use this exercise.

Witnessing mother kill my sister Instilled a lot of hatred, bitterness, fear, terror, horror, disease	Prompted me to look for ways I could help others, and in doing so, I became more compassionate towards others.
Enduring early childhood beatings I gained knowledge on the feelings of terror, rejection, fear and worthlessness, severe low self-esteem	Gave me insight into people's mental health. It helped me to look more philosophically at those times, leading me to self-help books to better understand
Bullied at School and home Caused me to have a short fuse with people. Through this, I adopted an ugly nature	Made me appreciate the times of respite when I would visit my aunties, uncles, and cousins. It also gave me strong armour to assist those in need
Racism within School Taught me a lot about separatism, cruelty, the ugly side of human nature	Prompted me to question the authority on the subject of racism throughout the ages
Drug abuse Understood my actions were that of a victim, acquired knowledge in the lack of self-respect, self-worth, and humiliation	Taught me about self-respect, self-worth, made me streetwise, taught me how to survive through self-abuse, and go on to teach the prevention of Drugs in schools and youth clubs

VACATION

"A vacation is what you take when you can no longer take what you've been taking."

[Earl Wilson]

If you don't have the cash ready to take a vacation, then go for the *'change is as good as a rest'* approach and set about doing things differently. Often times in the past, I would be locked inside my head with all sorts of turmoils. It was only when I made the decision to get out, do different things and the likes did I feel like I was having a break from what I allowed myself to become used to. When you try out new things, then you give your mind a break. It's like going on a vacation in mind; you have different experiences, meet different people, have different things to talk about and shed off the same old pattern. The more you try something new, the newer you become. Taking a mental vacation is as good as going on holiday, but without the drama of travel and flights. If, however, you are lucky enough to have the cash ready to go off and take a break, then it is important that you make a plan to do so as there is nothing like observing another environment. Even if it is just taking a few days out of your schedule, it has to be done for you to recharge your batteries. Vacations are adventures that leave us with hopefully good memories and raise our self-esteem.

Exercise: Write down 5 things that you would like to do that are different from what you are used to, then go do all 5 of them within the month.

CHAPTER 7

ASK

"He who is afraid to ask is ashamed of learning."

[Proverb]

"Ask and ye shall receive" does what it says on the tin. Usually, if you ask for something, you will receive an answer to what it is you are asking for. Having been a person that was too afraid to ask anyone for anything in my younger days, I truly understand how it can be a little nerve-racking to ask for what you want. There can be many different reasons why you fear to ask. Fast forward to today, and it's the total opposite. I now make a point of asking about anything that I don't know. My motto now is, if I don't understand, then I am going to make sure I ask someone that can help me to understand. It could be words, skills, information, etc. There is no shame in asking. If I don't know, then I will ask, and if there is no one to ask, then I will go within and ask my higher self. If it's the higher self, I am always guided to a situation that will lead me to the answer or I will be guided to someone that can reveal the answer to me.

We are lucky today that we have so many amazing sites online that can answer many of our not-so-personal questions, and I have caught myself asking Google for information that I know I will get a quick answer from. But what if you do not have a computer, or if you are in a situation that you know the computer will not be able to assist you with what you want? Asking is the only way forward for personal growth, become the ready student willing to learn what you do not know, and the teacher will appear one way or another. People love helping others with their knowledge, and they become truly helpful when sharing it with those who show an interest. Asking for help is a sign of strength. Benjamin Franklin once said, *"All highly competent people continually search for ways to keep learning, growing, and improving. They do that by asking WHY. After all, the person who knows HOW will always have a job, but a person who knows WHY will always be the boss."* Some people fear looking foolish by asking for something that will enhance their knowledge, but you hold yourself back when you don't ask so be brave and just ask, you would be foolish not to. Asking can also be an icebreaker and spark off conversations depending on what you are asking. If you don't ask, you don't get, and if you don't get, you don't grow. You can also ask yourself questions and almost instantly, intuition/higher self or whatever you want to call it always answers and usually with an answer that inspires you into action. Ask yourself the following question, "What is the one thing that I can do today that will get me closer to reaching my goal?" When the answer comes to your mind, write it down and then act upon it.

EXERCISE: If you are a person that finds it hard to ask for anything, then this exercise is about finding the courage to do so. Start off small by asking a complete stranger the time, watch how accommodating they are, as like I said before, people find joy in being able to assist others where they can. Ask someone for directions. Again, if they know, they will tell you, but if they do not, often times they might guide you onto the nearest shop for you to ask one of the locals. Write a list of 20 questions down that you may have always wanted answers to and place yourself in a position with people who might be able to assist you with finding the answers.

APPRECIATION

"When you lose everything, you get depressed if you don't step back and start appreciating what you do have."

[Paul and Tracey McManus]

To appreciate is to be grateful for, and to not appreciate what you have been given is to be ungrateful. When we are in an unappreciative mode, we attract more of the same. Appreciate all that you have, every experience, good or bad, for they are gifts passed your way to help strengthen you, especially what you perceive as being the really bad ones.

For years, I remained bitter about the way my mother brought me up in the periods that I was with her and not in a children's home. She was violent, brutal, cruel, bitter, and often spoke of her dislike for me. It is hard to appreciate that sort of upbringing, but appreciate it I do as, without question, it has made me into the person that I am today, and I really like being me. I often wonder what my life would have been like had I been brought up in what is deemed to be a normal household? I can tell you now that there is no way that I would have discovered what I now know growing up in normal surroundings. Now that I am older and have survived it all, I realise that what was passed my way not only didn't kill me, but it could also be used as a tool to help others who have been through similar circumstances. I changed the way I looked at my mother when I started delving deeper into her early childhood, which was pretty horrendous, to say the least. I became empathic about the whole thing and in doing so dissolved thoughts of bitterness and all that comes with that line of thinking. When I decided to appreciate my lot, it was like the scales had lifted from my eyes, and I started to attract more things in my life that made me appreciate further my past circumstances. I appreciate that my life's experiences have also enabled me to recognise my 'Life's Purpose,' which is now the thing that gets me out of bed each morning and makes me work on my 'SHOW & GROW' project aimed at assisting those who are stuck at a crossroads struggling to cope with their pain. There are many out there, and I appreciate that I now have the tools to assist each survivor. I realise that it might be hard to forgive someone for the wrongs that they may have done you, but if you do not look at it differently, then you will always be stuck in that mode of un-forgiveness, and what's more, those that have wronged you will have won, and you will never be able to appreciate what you actually have in terms of what you can do with that experience. I personally cannot let a past experience define me any longer as life is too short and I wish to live mine to the fullest, helping as many people on the way. I believe that if a person has gone through the traumas within their life, then they are in the know, and those who know teach, and those who teach experientially are best placed to help the human race evolve. Not only will it help them to cope with their past pains, but it will also make them appreciate how many people they can actually help with that knowledge. It is at that moment one is gently persuaded to look at the situation from a different perspective, taking it away from the 'I' or 'Me,' and when this is totally understood, then appreciation for what you have will show itself in all things. I have learnt to appreciate my lot, and as such, I now see that what I do have are actually the jewels in my crown and the tools to keep going and assist where I can; I LOVE that about me. **"Where there is no vision, there is no hope." [George Washington Carver]**

EXERCISE: You will need your pen and pad for this one as the exercise here is to write down what you feel you have learnt from those experiences, good and bad and really look at them as a tool that might be useful in helping others who have been through similar situations, for when you help others, you also help yourself. There are literally hundreds of groups out there crying out to listen to what you have to say through your experience, and if you feel brave enough, you can volunteer for one of these groups once a week, month, or fortnight. It is a must that you get involved, as only then will you appreciate that there will always be someone out there having gone through hardship that is waiting for someone like you to help them to keep going on.

AFFIRMATIONS

Optimistic affirmations regularly promote positive change within a person's life. I can vouch as a regular to this sort of exercise, this works 100% and is just so simple and easy. What you feed your mind goes on to serve you and how you wish to be served depends on what you feed your mind. The menu is vast and yours for the choosing. Many successful people and leaders make a point of choosing positive affirmations that they have running in the background while they get ready to start their day. They make a conscious effort to start their day with a powerful positive message for their mind, messages they know will stick with them for the rest of the day. Affirmations are best listened to first thing in the morning and last thing at night. When you repeat this daily, you are strengthening your mind's neural net to the point where it sticks and becomes your new way of thinking. When you do things repetitively, they sink into the psyche and are hard to shake off, so it's important that what you feed your mind is positive and conducive to your wellbeing. Every morning, I listen to the 'I AM' affirmations that I find on YouTube. I have my favourites that resonate with me, and it's up to you to find the ones that do the same for you. I have even taken to downloading some and adding them to the iPod so as I really thicken the neural net muscle. Think about it, when you were a child, you wore a nappy because you did not know yet how to go to the toilet. Eventually, after potty training and a few accidents, you managed to grasp that understanding. This has never left you; you do it regularly, and it has now stuck with you for life. When you feed your mind daily with something that will help you in the future, it will stay with you for life.

Exercise: Search the internet for daily affirmations; the I AM ones are usually the best ones as they replace all the negative thoughts that you come up with in your mind on a regular basis, such as “I am ugly,” “I am so stupid,” “I am an idiot,” etc. We all do it, but we have a choice to stop doing it by making a conscious effort to search for a better way of thinking. You can find affirmations for Health, Wealth, Happiness, Self-Love, Abundance; the list goes on. Once you have chosen a few, then download them and add them to your iPod or MP3 player if you have one. Or download them onto a CD or Pen-stick that can be played in your car on the way to work. I choose the ones that leave a space where I can repeat what is being said afterwards. I listen, then I copy word for word, and it works for me. Because I speak the affirmations, it becomes my way of thinking, and what I am doing is replacing the old thoughts with the new thoughts. I am a much better person for it, lighter, brighter, and far more positive. PLEASE try this exercise and apply it to your daily and evening routine; you will thank yourself for it.

ATTITUDE

"If you don't like something, change it. If you can't change it, change your attitude."

[Maya Angelou]

To survive this game called life, you just have to change your attitude. If you are the type of person that blames everyone but yourself for being the way you are or finding yourself in the circumstances that you're in, then you really have to take a look at your circumstances and get honest about how you have arrived there. People are usually where they are at any given moment because of the choices they make and because of their attitudes towards life. If you're the type of person that blames bad parenting, your environment, schooling, being bullied, abused, etc., linking them to your current circumstances, then know that this line of thought is severely holding you back from being the best that you can ever be; it's also delusional and an excuse from you allowing yourself to progress further.

At times I would go on about not having this or that because of bad parenting, growing up in poverty, coming from a violent background and all that did was to instil anger and bitterness within me. Being around negative and bitter people becomes a real pain, and most people will do what they can to avoid this sort of person. I was like it for years until I finally woke up. It may have been one of the many self-help books that finally kicked into my awareness of understanding that possibly inspired my change in attitude. I was able to observe how my own choices had got me to where I was. I found that by being truly honest with myself, I became more open to understanding truths I once denied. When you finally realise that unless you change your attitude of mind and stop blaming others for where you find yourself today, then nothing will change and you will remain on that treadmill of lack, woe is me, I can't do this because, etc. Blaming others or situations for where you are right now is foolish, it's a lazy way of thinking, it lacks substance, and it just holds you back from being the real you. A real change of attitude is needed to get you back on track with yourself and your reason for being; your attitude can either make you or break you. **"For success, attitude is equally as important as ability." [Walter Scott]**

EXERCISE: This exercise is all about being honest with yourself. Ask yourself the following questions: Once you have the honest answers, then act upon them to omit what is offensive and keep what is not. Work on your attitude towards people, life, and things.

- ✓ Do I have an attitude problem?
- ✓ Is my attitude toward people and life holding me back?
- ✓ Ask members of your family or friends what they think about your attitude?
- ✓ How many friends have I lost due to my attitude?
- ✓ Is my attitude towards life normal, and if not why not?

ASPIRE

"No matter what race or colour you are, you can aspire to do something great."

[Laurie Hernandez]

Aspire is in itself a very positive word. It is to rise to a greater height than the one you are currently at, to want to be something more than you are right now. Aspire to be the best version of yourself that you can be.

Draw a picture in your mind of how you wish to be. Include the people, surroundings, your health, personality, friendships, job, and finances. Aspire to have your talents shine, aspire to be a beacon of light for others, aspire to be the greatest role model that ever walked this planet, aspire to be a person so powerful that your very being enables those in power to make positive changes to outmoded ideas. Aspire to be someone that promotes positive change for yourself and others with the end game being to raise yours and their vibration, aspire to just be a great person all round. Having aspirations motivates a person into action, gets them out of bed in the morning, and sees them doing whatever they can to realise their dream of becoming the best that they can in their chosen field. **"Only if you aspire for more will you achieve more. [Chanda Kochhar]**

EXERCISE: Choose one thing that your heart resonates with and focus on building on this until you master it. This is an ongoing exercise until you become a master in that field. Aspire to be the best you can with what your heart truly resonates with.

ATTENTION

"The successful person places more attention on doing the right thing rather than doing things right."

[Peter F. Drucker]

Where does your attention lay? What is it you are paying attention to? Do you pay attention to your thoughts? What are they saying? How are they making you feel, what actions are you taking as a result of putting your attention on this one specific thing? Something as simple as what we put our attention on can make or break our day. Is your attention focused, or is it all over the shop?

Every morning, my attention is on my routine to get out of bed, shower, get ready, listen, and speak affirmations while getting ready to head to the gym with the full intention of coming back home and writing for at least an hour in my latest book. For a long time, my attention was focused in that area alone until one day, this rather lovely man started to take an interest in me. I couldn't help noticing him, and so for quite a few months, we had a non-physical or spoken relationship. It was quite exciting, and we both felt the attraction. However, what this did was to knock me off my usual attention on my morning routine, my attention when writing would suddenly go to an image of this man; it was almost like an obsession. It was silly because we had never even said hello to each other, but the chemistry was there when we passed each other or caught each other's eyes. My attention on my book slowed somewhat to make space for the new attention I had, that if I am honest, was not beneficial to my book other than explaining analogy. Eventually, the gym closed down for a refurbishment, and I went somewhere else where my attention on my book is back on par, and I am sailing through writing it. I, no doubt, might have finished it if I had not allowed myself to be distracted, steering my attention away from an initial focus on it. I recognise that when my attention is on more than one thing at a time, I am not in the present moment, and this causes my mind to be a tad chaotic. I do all that I can now to focus my attention on one thing at a time so that I can get the pure essence out of what it is I am paying my full attention to, and this has turned out to be fruitful.

Attention on others When someone talks to you, pay full attention to what they are saying, and if you catch your mind wandering off somewhere else, then bring your attention back to the person. If the person is a bore, then politely take your leave from the situation. If the person is saying something of importance, then give him/her your full attention for there is nothing more off-putting than for someone to give you their time in speech for you to avert your attention elsewhere. "**Whatever you focus your attention on will become more important to you even if it's unimportant.**" **[Sonya Parker]**

EXERCISE: First thing in the morning, write 2 things that you would most like to put your attention on doing that will benefit your future. Choose one for the morning and one for the afternoon and then proceed. I guarantee that someone or something will happen for your attention to be taken away for a moment in time. If you are a writer like me, then pop-ups on the computer are distracting and often I find that I allow them to take my attention away from what it is I am doing. All of that can be avoided when we make up our mind to become 'attention-specific.' I now choose my attention for my whole morning to be on my book and nothing else. I turn all my phones down, don't answer emails, ignore pop-ups and just keep my attention on the prize, which is my book. Your exercise is to choose two things that will benefit your future growth and give separate time to each so as you can build upon the ideas you have for them. Make a decision to put at least an hour on each with 100% full attention, and after a week, you will not believe how much you have built. Try it, you will amaze yourself, and more importantly, you will respect what mastering your attention can do for you in your life and the lives of others.

AVOID

"Do not worry about avoiding temptation. As you grow older, it will avoid you."

[Joey Adams]

It seems that I have spent my recent years avoiding the things that no longer serve my highest self and I have become such a dab hand at it all now that it has become part of my person and something that many of my true friends appreciate me for. I simply LOVE being known for what I have become in relation to what I once was. Many years ago, my then low self-esteem would find me in situations that I was too frightened to avoid just in case of any conflict. Fear stopped me from speaking up for myself, and so I would just go with the flow or follow suit for possible peace and quiet. This, of course, was backward thinking, given the company I was choosing to keep around those times. I am happy to say that, today, I have rules and those rules are to avoid absolutely everything that lowers my vibration; simple. I call it one of my greatest strengths. Saying no or just choosing to avoid something because it does not fit in with my plan of positivity can actually be quite liberating, especially when you become well known for it. I have gone from meek to seriously powerful in my resolve. As an addict, it was hard to avoid the dark side as I was part of the fabric, but as time went on and it became apparent to me that if I didn't stop, then I would most certainly die. The one major thing I had going for me was willpower and the courage to avoid anyone stopping me from getting out of that situation and back to health again. It took a while, but I did it, and that's all because I chose to avoid what once was. I now feel completely comfortable in my own skin having applied this rule. I have done it since with past friends who have consistently shown their negative side aimed at bringing me down. I usually delete these people from my phone, emails, social media sites, and in this way, I avoid anything more to do with them. I also do it in a loving way; recently I had to let a past friend go as her actions toward me were appalling, to say the least. That night, I made a decision to cut her totally out of my life and so, that way, I avoid seeing or knowing any more about her. In my head, I wished her the very best in life and thanked her for the experiences thus far, but I also said that I no longer want to be involved with people being negative towards me. I am happy with that decision, and if perchance I do bump into her in the street, I will not be rude should she manage to say hello, but I will avoid full conversation, plus any invite or association. This action frees me up to experience more positive people in my life. **"If you want to attract goodness into your life, then avoid what does not resonate with your heart, mind, body and soul and replace it with that which does." [Jennie Matthias]**

EXERCISE: Write a list of all things that make you feel uneasy for whatever reason and do all you can to avoid them. Again, do this one by one as doing it separately strengthens your reasoning behind avoiding what you no longer want in your life.

ACTION

"Personal power is the ability to take action."

[Tony Robbins]

In life, there are talkers and doers. Talkers are the ones who talk about what they want to do, but usually keep on talking about it without ever actually doing it; then there are the doers who see something they want to do and just go ahead and do it. To do is to act, and actions speak louder than words. To act upon an idea is to be disciplined, and to act upon it immediately is to get a result of some kind or other. The history books are full of people who have had incredible ideas but not acted upon them only to find a few weeks, months, or years down the line that someone else had a similar idea, acted upon it, and became highly successful in doing so. If an excellent idea pops into your head, know that this is a gift that has been given to you to act upon and not put on the shelf for a later date. When that idea is put on the shelf, preparing it for a rainy day, then you have lost all the momentum, and the original light bulb spark fizzles out. Jim Rohn said, "The time to act is when the iron is hot and the emotion is strong." I cannot count the number of people that say, Jennie, I want a figure like yours, what do you do to keep in that sort of shape? When I tell them that my daily routine requires that I leave my bed at 4:30 - 5.00 am each morning to be in the gym for an hour and a half workout, I always get the reply or words to the effect of, "Are you crazy? I can't do that," to which I usually say "Well, you won't get a figure like mine then." One day I looked in the mirror and didn't like what I saw, so I made a decision to act upon changing what I didn't like. Now, I am in the gym 5 - 6 times a week before 6:00 am and I see the results as do others. Because I took action, I have knocked 10 years off of my look, have the body on a 25-year-old and have more stamina than ever. I now look in the mirror, and my vision of me is 100% more positive about my body than it was before taking action. I had a burning desire to lose a stone and a half, I have achieved that, made new friends at the gym and the early mornings mean that I can write on my books for longer. The content created early in the morning seems to be much easier and flows better. Taking immediate action on a good idea will give you an inner power. I now walk down the road, and I feel amazing that over the past two years, I have now got the body I dreamed of having; result. So, whether an idea is big or small, the key is to act upon it straight away. If the idea comes when you are at work, then write some notes down. As soon as you have finished work, find a place where you can add to those ideas and then prepare the time for you to act upon it.

Exercise: Go out and buy a journal specifically for jotting down any idea that you have. Now, think of something that you would like to do; it could be a new job, become self-employed, learn how to play an instrument, bake a cake, learn how to swim, etc. Whatever it is, it has to be something that you have always wanted to do, but have always made an excuse not to do it. Now write down that one thing and act upon making it happen. You may have to sacrifice something else in order to act upon that which you desire, but the idea here is just to ACT and then when you have mastered that action, go on to take action on something else until taking action becomes part of your make-up. The results will speak for themselves, and you will become extremely powerful from within when you experience the results and achievements due to your very own actions. People who act upon what they say that they will do also get the respect of all those who observe those actions. - FACT!

ACCEPTANCE

"Happiness can only exist in acceptance."

[George Orwell]

It is hugely important for us to accept the things we cannot change, for if we do not accept them, then we unknowingly hold ourselves back from moving forward. What is done is done, and it cannot be changed, but you can change how you respond to it. To not accept is to live a lie, to live in denial, hiding from what is, which in turn lowers our vibration. It also means that we are unable to let go of that which we do not accept to be true. When we accept what is and has been, we free ourselves from the chains of denial, leaving room for new discoveries about life that will lift us up and eventually dissolve the demons we have spent so much time denying. My mother's violent behaviour towards me took years to get over. The worst abuse of all, however, was when I became self-abusive, which came in the form of taking class A drugs. I believe I did this as a way of escaping my demons brought on by those early actions. I was bitter, angry, and uncomfortable with what I had become, but still in denial about my past experiences having any effect on me. It was ugly to view my daily demise; my habits were literally killing me. Thank goodness that I was guided to the right books and people that became an integral part of my cleaning up, and in doing so, I just decided to accept what had been done to me and what I had done to myself. I began to accept that what had been done was now history, and rather than complaining, feeling bitter and angry than to just accept it for what it is would be the best thing to do. I figured that since I had never tried to just accept how my life had been, it was time I did something different with my understanding of all this. Soon after accepting that I cannot change what was, I felt a freeing in my mind. It was slight, but I did feel it, and it made me think about things differently. I started to become different and obtained a hard-to-explain inner power. I just knew it was time for me to move on from what had been holding me back for years. That one act of acceptance escalated into other areas of my life, especially relationships with friends or those that would see me as an enemy or vice versa. I don't see people as enemies anymore as I have taught myself to accept them for who and what they are. I have been able to accept some truly crazy things as of late just because I now recognise the power of acceptance. I now realise that my Mother did what she did out of ignorance and inner rage brought over from her equally abusive childhood, and although that does not make what she did right, I do understand why she did it, and in doing so, I accept it with complete gratitude and LOVE. It's now been years and, like I say, I have moved on because the power of accepting is so much more powerful than that of denial. If you've had an argument with someone and it's still with you days later, then do the best thing for you; drop it. If you are still living the memory of the past and it plays out in your head like an old black and white movie, then try to accept that you have become attached to the experience and also accept that you are allowing the past to affect your future. What's past is past, and each time you bring an old wound up, you bring it back to life. It's almost like you cannot accept that it's gone, so you press replay in your mind. The moment you accept the past for what it is and that it is now history, then your future will present many new doors for you to enter. You start to raise your vibration and attract more high vibration things. When you refuse to accept what is, you remain stuck in the old movie running on a low vibration where you will also attract that which does not benefit you in the long run.

EXERCISE: Write down what is niggling you at the moment. Is there something that really gets your blood boiling, whether it be from the past or maybe a recent argument? Whatever that is, it is damaging to you if it makes you feel uncomfortable. These are the sort of things to write in your list, go through them one by one and change your thought about them. Do what you can to look at them from a different perspective. Look at each one and mentally repeat that you now accept that what has happened cannot be undone. If it was an abusive parent, then look at the situation again, forgive and then accept that what happened cannot be changed. Write it on a piece of paper, ***"I now accept what has happened cannot be changed and I am okay with that."*** Scrunch it up and then free yourself from that past moment by burning the paper. This adds weight to your action of acceptance. Turn it into an offering for the self. I now accept what I cannot change and would like to move on so that I can enjoy my life and be free. It is what it is and was what it was, and I am now what I am despite what was. Go down the list and do each one separately and free yourself from each dark moment by replacing it with accepting things as they are. You can try this in one day or night, but I prefer to take a day or night at a time and reflect on that positive action until I find myself smiling about the situation rather than getting mad. After you have done all this, then meditate with gratitude in your heart that you are now accepting things the way they are. If you do this with genuine forgiveness in your heart, then all I can say is watch and evidence the miracles that will follow.

CHAPTER 8

LEARN

"Anything that hurts you can teach you, and if it keeps hurting you, it's because you haven't learned."

[Anonymous]

If you think that you learnt something of true worth in school, then you are sadly mistaken, nothing prepares you for real life. The moment you leave school is where your true lessons start, and from there onwards, your responsibility. You become the teacher and also the pupil. If you mess up, then it's only you to blame and here starts your very first life lesson.

Life is a game of chance, risk, opportunity, choice, circumstances, and various situations, and it's how we respond to all those that determines how fast or slow we reach our destination. On this new journey where you are now accountable for all of your actions, you will no doubt take many risks. But you will also be offered many opportunities, and throughout life, you will be given numerous chances. You are given the tools of experience to fashion out something for yourself to assist your survival; how you use these tools is down to you and a matter of choice.

Many have often failed, succeeded, and then failed again. This is all good as not only are you collecting life experiences that you might be able to use in the future, but it is an important part of the lessons that would need to be learnt for you to totally understand where it is you are heading. Not everyone gets to the end of their destination, but those who do usually accrue an eclectic mix of experiences, enabling them to form a hard exterior, which you will need to have so that you make it through the hard-knocks areas that will help shape your future. The harder the lesson, the larger the growth. Once you have fully understood that lesson, you move onto the next, and the choice is yours on how fast or slow that may be. We each have a destination, and we all have a choice to walk down whatever path we choose to reach it. Some allow themselves to get distracted and so do a detour, leading them astray and away from their objective. This may come in the form of drugs, drink, promiscuity, over-working, addictions, etc., but it is still OK as every area of life that you indulge your time in is a lesson worth learning. Those who know grow in knowledge; Knowledge is Power.

Once you go through whatever it is you have to go through, whether it be loss, pain, abuse, failure, rejection, grief, etc., and if you manage to survive all or any of these, then you are actually allowing yourself to become the best version of you that you can be. The more challenging the experience, the deeper the lesson, and in time will gain the wisdom to teach others. However, you will not be able to do any of this if you refuse to learn from the lessons you set yourself up for. Life is all about learning how to LOVE yourself and others, and within our lives, we have as many bad times as well as good and these are needed to assist you in understanding fully the balance of life. Once you get it on the deepest level, you will change your course and get back on the right track.

Exercise: If you are weak in an area of your life, then search the internet for how to overcome that weakness. Search for how others have overcome their weaknesses, you will find that you are not alone in this area and so by actively searching for ways to strengthen the parts of you that are weaker than others, you are sending a message to the universe that you are willing to master or learn how to better that part of you. There are millions of people that will have done what they could to overcome their weaknesses, seek them out and learn from them; I did and so can you. I remember a friend of mine was severely dyslexic, but he made himself read books. He was also an actor and reading scripts did not come easily to him, so he developed a way of learning off by heart very quickly, and he was very good at it. If there is an area that you feel there is something that you wish you had learnt more of, then pick one and master it. It can be writing a book, playing an instrument, learning a different language, it has to be something that you WANT to do, and I emphasise the WANT as it is very important that you love what it is that you learn. The idea is to do all you can to master that one thing, and you will find along the way that you will meet new people in the field of your chosen lesson. For example, I really wanted to be a Public Speaker but had never delved into that area. Anyway, I saw something online inviting me to an 'Andy Harrington' seminar, where a Public Speaking Academy was being promoted to all who attended. I felt so inspired I joined up for the course, and in doing so, I met a whole new bunch of people that I am still in touch with today. We are in a 'WhatsApp' group, and we are constantly inspiring each other. We also hold meetings and share our daily, weekly, or monthly achievements to the whole group. When you embark on a new venture, new things start to happen along with new friends made. It really is a big beautiful world out there, especially when you make the choice to learn something new. I remember wanting to know how to learn computers when they came out because I didn't want to be left behind. I was already a good, fast typist, but I couldn't grasp the computer. I enrolled in a course where there were X amount of people in the same boat, and as such, we would all encourage each other to get on. Now I am computer savvy, and my friends that didn't venture down that road are now reliant on others helping them to do the simplest task. When you take on a new form of training or learning, you not only gain new skills, but you broaden your horizons further. Learning becomes quite addictive if what you learn is what you actually LOVE or is something that you can foresee as being beneficial to your future. So the exercise is just to find one thing and do all you can to master it. Anthony J. D'Angelo once said, *'Develop a passion for learning. If you do, you will never cease to grow.'*

"Live as if you were to die tomorrow. Learn as if you were to live forever."

[Mahatma Gandhi]

LAUGHTER

"No matter what your heartache may be, laughing helps you forget it for a few seconds."

[Red Skelton]

They say that laughter is the best medicine, which begs the question, why do we need so many doctors then? People have been known to heal themselves with this one simple act. Laughter is the best drug on the market, and what's more, it is FREE. The upside is that there is no downside and it has no negative effects. It's positively contagious, and there are NO comedowns. It has also been known to cure inner and outer pain, which could well be due to that extra endorphin rush one gets when one laughs. When you laugh, the whole world laughs with you, and everything seems so much brighter. Remember, no one wants to be around a moody person. Laughter helps raise vibration in an instant, and when your vibration is raised, then you are in alignment to attract all that is positive towards you. It is the law of the universe that we attract what we are, and if we are happy, then we will attract more of the same. No wonder people are actively using it as an alternative to conventional medicine as a way to cure their ills. Laughter is known to release good brain chemicals and prompts an increase in endorphins. To laugh with someone or even a group is to bond with them in such a genuine way and brings you even closer to that person. I have been known to start my mornings with having a comedy audio running in the background as I am getting ready for the gym. It's a priceless way to start the day in fits of laughter. I am a great believer in starting the day with a smile or a side-splitting laugh. It's a significant part of my routine, and I am always being invited out just because I know how to have fun and am not ashamed to laugh. If people made laughter part of their daily agenda, my guess is that the world may be positively different today. I personally think it should be added to the school curriculum; I am not kidding. Mark Twain once said, *"Against the assault of laughter nothing can stand."*

EXERCISE: Find 30 comedy videos, and if you are in a position to download them, then even better. Start your day with listening to just one every day for a month and see how different your days, weeks, and month is by this simple act. Just run it in the background while you're getting ready for work, or even better still, if you can download it onto your iPod, then you can play it while you're travelling. You may get some strange looks on the tube though, but hey, who cares, you might never see those people again. Also, if they see you laughing, they will also laugh and that, my friend, is what life's all about; creating a happy environment for all.

LOVE

"Love is the only force capable of transforming an enemy into a friend."

[Martin Luther King, Jr.]

There is not a person alive who would be able to survive without Love. Love is the only thing we strive in this life to be and have, but many do not experience its true worth. Love is deep, and we are here because of that deep love. To love, be loved, and to spread that love is our only mission. Love is born of God and the Goddess, and we are born of love. Love is the father and the mother, love is all there is; we are the children of divine LOVE. When we are not in love or experiencing its true essence, then we are not in alignment with ourselves or the planet, which causes us to experience disharmony from within. In order for us to understand the meaning of love fully, we have to also understand and experience its opposite; hate. You cannot experience LOVE without a measure of its opposite. Pain and hatred are the catalyst to understanding true love and its importance to you, the planet, and its inhabitants.

Throughout my lifetime and especially in the early stages, I experienced a lot of hatred and rejection from my Mother. She was violent, cruel, and her temper would always be taken out on me as I was the oldest. In those times, I experienced the opposite of love, but when I was lucky enough to go into a Children's home, I experienced love [the opposite of hate] from the likes of Auntie Alice and from some of the people who lived there. I would also get visits from my Uncle, and my favourite was going to visit my

Auntie Nada. She was a wonderful, caring lady with an open heart who understood what we were going through. It was always hard to leave her as she would show us so much love and I always felt that she was sad to see us go back into that environment. When you are brought up in an environment that is surrounded by darkness, you appreciate more the times when those around you are just ready to love you like they would their own child. To truly appreciate love is to know its opposite (which is to have experienced a world without love), and when we truly appreciate something, we are acting in the mode of gratitude. To be grateful is to love and appreciate. This is the place where our soul feels calm and peaceful, and it is also a lesson learnt.

Dr Bruce Lipton says: "LOVE FEEDS CELLS," so taking that into consideration, all we have to do is look at how we react to being hungry and how uncomfortable that feels. But when we are fed, it makes us feel good and keeps us going. Love nourishes us in a way that food does not; love is of the heart. Now that we know love feeds cells, it would be wise to bear that in mind when we are surrounded by people that do not love us or we have an aversion to. Sometimes and certainly in the case of my mother, I have walked away, and in my heart and mind have wished her the best without no malice while also choosing to move on and pursue relationships and friendships that were more conducive to my wellbeing. There comes a time when you just have to move on from that sort of environment and look for greener pastures. When I came of age, I did just that and have never looked back. So the moral of this is that LOVE is the most important thing in your life, and if you do not have it now, then you will have to make a point of making sure that you experience it within your lifetime, even if it is just once. It's OK if you have just gone through the loss of a loved one, or you are now an ex-boyfriend or girlfriend, this is all part of the experience of life that we must all practice in order to grow into our greater selves and realise the truth about LOVE. When friends are going through the sadness of a broken relationship, I always encourage them to look at the bigger picture. "It is better to have loved and lost than never to have loved at all." It is in those times, when we are in the most painful situations, that we appreciate what we once had and the aftermath of those times and the journey thereafter offers its own wisdom depending on how you cope with the situation at hand. LOVE is truly what we all strive for because, to put it simply, LOVE is all there is and it is the biggest weapon we have against its opposite.

Exercise: Look in the mirror and ask yourself the following questions:

Do I love me? My job? My environment? My friends? My life? If all your answers are yes, then you are a very lucky person who will hopefully be very grateful for having all that you require in life. If, on the other hand, you find areas that you do not love about yourself, environment, friends, situations, then do all that you can to omit the things that you do not love about them and strengthen your area of LOVE. Learn to truly LOVE yourself, and in doing so, you will also experience others falling in love with you.

LIVING

"A life without cause is a life without effect."

[Barbarella]

Are you living your life the way you would like? Are you enjoying yourself within it? You know you're living your life on purpose when you cannot wait to get out of the bed to work on your life's mission. To explore the unknown, to mould the day and week to fit your agenda. When the day ahead looks so exciting that you just cannot wait to take it on and when you do it with a view to obtaining results, then that is living. When you feel that sense of achievement, it just raises your energy and vibration, for you are well aware that you are heading the right way, you are happy with your lot, and you are grateful for another day in which to expand on your dreams. When the tasks that you have set out for yourself to achieve are accomplished, it just feels great, and that is truly living on purpose.

If, on the other hand, you find yourself doing the opposite, where you hit the snooze button and start your day wishing that you can have a day off to stay under the covers and do literally nothing, then that is certainly an area of your life you need to look at. If you are dragging yourself to a job you are not passionate about, fearful of what the day may bring, if you have a task that looks daunting to you, something that you have to confront that you would rather not, then it is up to you to sort that area of your life out, as doing anything that goes against your happiness will result in you feeling uncomfortable or uneasy. When you feel uneasy, your feelings will show you that you are out of alignment with the universe. If what you are feeling is not in harmony with your being, then you will have to eventually look into how you can reverse that as living with dissonance is not living your life in harmony. Nathaniel Branden once said, "Every day, it's important to ask and answer these questions: ***"What's good in my life?"*** and ***"What needs to be done?"***

EXERCISE: Write these six categories in your journal like I have done below and honestly ask yourself the following questions:

Love Life - "Am I truly happy in this relationship?"

Job - "Does this job inspire me to get out of bed early?"

Environment - "Do I see myself here in 5 years?"

Friends - "Am I allowing some of my friends to hold me back from living my dreams?"

Family - "Am I allowing family members to get to hold me back from living my life?"

Habits - "Are my habits stunting my growth, stopping me from living my true potential?"

LIFE'S PURPOSE

Two years ago, I had never heard of a 'Life's Purpose,' and if someone had asked me then if I knew what my one was, I would simply not have been able to answer them. I was totally ignorant about its meaning and its importance, not only in my life, but others also. I am 61 years of age, and one would have thought that by now I would have had some sort of idea about it.

From what I understand, a 'Life's Purpose' is a person's reason to be, their soul's mission, and it is indeed the thing that keeps them going day after day. I have performed at a few poetry events as of late, and one of the poems I created has a lot to do with how I have arrived at what I now know as my 'Life's Purpose.' Within the poem, I briefly share the story of my harsh upbringing and explain to the listener how each experience has not only made me who I am today, but it has also enabled me to become an authority on how to survive the world of hard knocks to where I am able to embrace it all in a positive manner and share my findings with those that have gone through similar hardship. I always start this poem off by asking the audience if they know what their 'Life's Purpose' is and to my surprise, none of them knew what I was talking about. Not only did that shock me, but I felt that it was important to look further into why people have not ever really ventured into the importance of finding theirs. If you don't have a purpose, a mission, a clear vision for where you are heading, then how do you know where you are going? I feel that my 'Life's Purpose' is to encourage people how to find theirs and I do this by sharing mine in the hope that this will inspire others to achieve their aims on this earth. I have a strong belief that we are all here for a reason and each and every one of us has a mission on this earth. It seems that the majority of us take years to realise this and some even go to their graves never knowing that they came here for a purpose.

Entrepreneur Adam Leipzig made a discovery when he attended a high school reunion. He observed that 80% of his old school mates had gone on to become wealthy and seemed to have two of everything but were not happy and at a loss to figuring out what their life's purpose was, and the other 20% who had figured out their life's purpose were happy because of the following five attributes. They knew:

- who they were
- what they did
- who they did it for
- what those people wanted or needed
- what they got out of it and how they changed as a result

Adam went on to say that Amazon listed 151,928 books on the subject of people finding their 'Life's Purpose.' He also went into more detail about how you can also find your 'Life's Purpose' by asking the following questions:

Who are you? - [your name]

What do you like to do? [what is the one thing that you feel highly qualified to teach people?]

Think about who you are doing it for. [Paint a picture in your mind of who that might be]

What do the people want or need that they can give them this one thing?

How do they change as a result of you being able to give them with that one thing?

Now that I know my 'Life's Purpose,' Adam's words above make pure sense to me, and my only regret is that I had not known or understood this earlier in my life, for had I known, then I would have certainly been in a more favourable position at a younger age. But no matter, I now know it, and there will be NO turning back from it. It was only when attending a few seminars did I realise that notes I had been taking throughout my life were being done in preparation for me to use once I had discovered my 'Life's Purpose.' I attended an Andy Harrington Seminar where he spoke about turning your Passion Into Profit, and it was such an eye-opener for me that I have never looked back and have expanded on all those notes and creations, turning them into something that I feel will assist the human race in so many positive ways.

I created the SURVIVE poem to share with those who might resonate with its content and, believe me, there have been many in the audiences I have recited this poem to that have immediately been inspired into acting upon looking into their 'Life's Purpose' or simply wanting to just ask more questions about it. The poem depicts both dark and light emotions and was written as a problem solution piece aimed at inspiring and empowering those who are struggling to cope with life's many pains and traumas. I hope that when you read the SURVIVE poem in this book, that it may encourage you to look at your circumstance at a deeper level, with the view to inspiring you to create something of worth from your own life's experiences.

EXERCISE: Look back on your life and take notes about every occasion you can remember. It's best to write them in a journal specifically for this purpose as you can always read them on the way to work and expand on the content. You will find that as you delve into the past, a door within your mind will open up those forgotten memories; good and bad, all need to be written down. Once you have exhausted all this, then look at where you are now in your life and ask yourself those 5 questions that Adam asked his audience. Once you look at where you have been and what you have experienced coupled with some highly intelligent questions, you will be on your way to finding your 'Life's Purpose.' And once you find it, you will not look back, as it will be the thing that inspires you into action for the rest of your life. If you're stuck, then do read my poem again as it speaks a truth that many can relate to. It is a personal journey into how I have arrived at where I am today and will kick start you into action. Everyone has a personal story, one that needs to be shared so that others can learn from your experience.

CONCLUSION

Millions of people go through traumatic experiences, and each of them has a story to tell, but few of them use that story to help themselves or others. I believe that these experiences are gifts passed our way to help strengthen us so that we can become the person we initially set out to be. We are all here for a purpose and maybe, just maybe, those traumatic moments of time were actually blessings in disguise to offer us insight into our reason for being positioning us on the path of discovering our *life's purpose*.

No one has to be defined by what one person thinks of them; no one. Life is all about the choices we make. We can choose to be happy or choose to be sad, it really is that simple. We cannot change the past, but we can create for ourselves a better future. We can be the light for a new generation, and we can be their hope for lifetimes to come. History is full of harrowing stories, some worse than others and the internet is awash with untold success stories depicting tales of people going through hell and back and coming out the other side. People who are using their survival experiences to help those struggling to cope with past traumas.

If you are still alive to tell the tale, then you are in the most powerful position to help the human race evolve. You now have the tools to positively raise a person's vibration. You are worth so much more than you have been led to believe. You have the knowledge to create a better world and the only thing holding you back is the person staring back at you in the mirror. You have the knowledge and the power to change school policies. Remember, every ordeal you have endured was actually a gift to help strengthen you, to help you grow so that you can then go on to show others how they too can do the same. You are a powerful teacher, a guide, a warrior of this universe, and you now have the credentials to be a voice for the voiceless. Know your worth and build on it, hang with other like-minded people that have gone through similar hardships and are finding ways of using those experiences to help those in need with a view to changing the world. Trawl through the internet and observe the many people doing extraordinary things with their experiences. These same people are not only helping millions of folks to find their full potential, but they are becoming financially stable in the process. There is a plethora of books, videos, YouTube clips, etc., that can be observed at the click of a button. Get involved, and go to seminars on these subjects. Look up the likes of Andy Harrington, Michelle Watson, Tony Robbins, the list is endless and get inspired into action. Now that you know you are of the greatest worth to people and this planet, what's holding you back? There is no more time for excuses, they just hold you back. Action is what is needed *now*, so get involved and change the world and your world for the better.

BIBLIOGRAPHY

(Books that have helped me on my journey)

Feeling is The Secret - Neville Goddard

You can Heal Your Life - Louise Hay

Conversations with God - Neale Donald Walsh

The Power Of Positive Thinking - Norman Vincent Peale

Celestine Prophecy - James Redfield

As a Man Thinketh - James Allen

God on a Harley - Joan Brady

The Secret - Rhonda Byrne

The Monk Who Sold His Ferrari - Robin Sharma

Think and Grow Rich [Original Edition] - Napoleon Hill

Awakened Imagination - Neville Goddard

Passion Into Profit - Andy Harrington

The Way of The Peaceful Warrior - Dan Millman

Breakthrough Experience - Dr F. Demartini

INSPIRATIONAL PEOPLE THAT HAVE HELPED ME ON MY JOURNEY

Tom Bilyeu (Impact Theory)
Neale Donald Walsh
Jim Rohn
Jesus' life
Wayne Dyer
Norman Vincent Peale
Napoleon Hill
Andrew Carnegie
Maya Angelou
Louise Hay
Delores Cannon
Neville Goddard
Michelle Watson
Andy Harrington
Buddha
Dr Akong Rinpoche
Gregg Braden
Dr Joe Dispenza
Bruce Lipton
Les Brown

This book is dedicated to the following people who have had a positive influence on my life.

Nurse Bruton and Sister Mary Theresa from the convent who showed compassion towards me. My late Aunty Nada and Uncle Papa who were always welcoming when I was in need of respite from those dark years, you taught me that there was love in this world for me and I shall never forget you both. Aunty Alice from the children's home in Slough who showed me the importance of having stability in my life taught me to have impeccable manners and encouraged me to read and write, though she was also strict, it was always done with love. Mrs Ashton-Jinks, who instilled in me the importance of learning new words and studying, left me with amazing advice that I still use today. Polly Perkins, who believed in my athletic skills and though I didn't always remember that, you were a person who believed that I could make it, and so I hope that I am making you proud now wherever you are in this universe. Theresa Caulfield, my very best friend at secondary school, whose family would always take me in when I could not stand another beating at home. My life would have been so different now if you and your family had not taken me in at the times when you did and the fact that we are still friends after all these years speaks volumes. Aunty Mayla, for taking me in at a crucial time in my teens after running away from home and doing your very best to show me the ropes. I shall never forget your kindness Mayla. William Farquhar, my first real boyfriend for always encouraging me to do what I can to get to the next stage and for never judging me in my darker days. To Christopher Foreman, not just an ex-boyfriend, but a true dear friend who has pulled me out of numerous financial situations in order to keep my head above water. You have been an angel in my life. Ged Forrest, for never letting me down when it comes to me needing my works edited at quick speed. Your intelligence, quick wit, and generosity with your time are very much appreciated in my life. Adrian Sherwood for being my brother from another mother, for always encouraging me to just go for it, for never judging me and for taking me under his wing when I was ready to throw the towel in on life, still giving me sound advice today. Shauna O'Briain, for allowing me to be your mentor and making me so very proud of what you have since achieved. To Michelle Watson, for mentoring me and believing in me, and being the only person on the planet to inspire me enough to write my first ever book and finish it. An extra special thank you has to go to my mother, Margaret McKeown, who I honestly believe I chose as a parent knowing that I would endure her wrath for most of my childhood. I believe that I did this with a view to learning the lessons I have since learnt from being in a situation like that. Over the years, I have come to appreciate the negativity, beatings, and harsh words thrown my way as it has made me the person I am today. For this, I appreciate that you have sacrificed much so that I can share my knowledge of those times with others. Thank you, Margaret, and I wish you only love and happiness wherever you are in the universe. Madscotsman Media, for getting my work out to the masses on a professional level and creating the image design for the cover of this book.

HARD TIMES ARE ONLY TEMPORARY

(Famous people that overcame adversity)

Nick Vujicic, a motivational speaker born with no arms and legs. He doesn't let anything get him down and is married to the love of his life.

Ed Sheeran was severely bullied in his early years and is now one of the biggest stars on the planet.

Comedian Jim Carrey once lived out of a VW camper van and in a tent on his sister's front lawn, and is one of the most famous actors in Hollywood.

Oscar winner, Halle Berry, who once stayed in a homeless shelter in her early 20s is now a very famous actress.

Talk show host, Dr Phil, who once lived in a car with his father, is now a famous talk show host.

Daniel Craig, who once had to sleep on park benches in London, is now James Bond.

Singer Ella Fitzgerald was homeless before becoming the 'Queen of Jazz.'

Albert Einstein didn't speak until he was four years old.

Kris Carr turned her cancer into a business of hope and healing.

Franklin Roosevelt became partially paralysed at 39.

Charlize Theron, who witnessed her mother kill her father, is now a model/actress.

Eminem suffered a brutal childhood attack, then used it as creative material to share with the masses.

Rihanna was bullied by her peers because of the colour of her skin.

Helen Keller was the first deaf-blind person to earn a Bachelor of Arts degree.

Mozart was deaf, but that never stopped him composing and becoming the genius he became.

"STORMS DON'T LAST FOREVER"

20059254R00113

Printed in Great Britain
by Amazon